fe

by

Ann Whitaker

Giving Life A Go

by

Ann Whitaker

Publisher
Best Books Online
Mediaworld PR Ltd

Copyright 2004

First paperback edition published in Great Britain
April 2004 by
Best Books Online
Mediaworld PR Ltd

ISBN 1-904502-47-4

1004717086 T

I am dedicating this story to my dear Mum.
In recognition of all the hard work and love
she has given me throughout my life.

GOD BLESS YOU
MUM.

Audrey Whitaker
passed away on 28th April 2003
RIP

Foreword

My name is Ann Whitaker.

I am writing my story so that anyone who is born like me would have the chance to benefit and achieve what I thought was impossible.

I was born in December 1964 and diagnosed Cerebral Palsy, 'Athetoid'. This meant that my body was rigid and all my movements jerky and uncontrollable. My parents have told me that when I was three months old they realised that something was drastically wrong. They took me to see a paediatrician, who told them: "Put her in a home – she will be a cabbage. Forget about her, she will never walk or talk."

Since then my parents have taken me to specialists from Leeds to London, not one of them gave any help or advice. The same story again and again – "Put her in a home."

They devoted their lives to helping me all they could, knowing I was mentally alert, trapped in a twisted body. No doctor or specialist would allow me to have any treatment on the National Health; consequently my parents knew they had to 'go it alone'.

Over the years they paid for physiotherapy, speech therapy, hydrotherapy, horse riding and swimming. From the age of five I attended a school for the physically handicapped, where I was treated as a normal human being with only a physical disability.

At the age of ten I went to a boarding school for physically handicapped girls. Throughout my school years I only made very slow progress, never reaching the potential my parents expected. My parents then moved from Yorkshire to Hampshire and I came to live at home. They found a local physiotherapist who came once a week; she was called Elizabeth.

After a few years I wanted to make my own way in life with other young handicapped people. My parents never stopped looking for anything new to help me. Elizabeth suggested trying the

Alexander Technique with Mr Bob Donovan, near where I was living. He treated me once a week for two years and this helped my body to relax as it had never done before.

Mr Donovan came to see my parents. He was quite excited – he had been on a seminar in London where he had met Mr Peter Blythe, who gave a lecture on a treatment he had given children at Chester. He asked us if we would meet Mr Blythe, as his treatment might help me. We decided that I should go and have an assessment.

Mr Blythe asked my parents questions about my treatment and early years. He seemed to know all about it before they had time to answer, and while they talked, he was watching me too. He was kind and understanding, knowing how embarrassed I felt with my jerky movements and speech difficulties.

After another assessment with his partner, Joan Young, Mr Blythe told me that he could improve the quality of my life. He gave me a daily exercise programme to be carried out at home, telling us it would be hard work for us all, and that dad would get fed up with driving to Chester every six weeks!

I have been on the treatment now for three years. The progress I have made is unbelievable – not only physically, but mentally too. I find now that when I am with people I don't feel embarrassed because, with the improvement in my speech, they understand what I say without my having to repeat myself and I no longer have the jerky movements which restricted me and gave me so much embarrassment.

I find the only way I can explain the difference the treatment has made is this – I always felt I had a spring wound tight inside me, now that spring has wound down.

I continued to progress over the next year of treatment but I was beginning to feel restless and knew I had to find somewhere to live where I could be with people of my own age and make a future for myself. I knew my Mum and Dad were getting very tired.

I have now found a lovely family home with my own room and have made many friends, the lovely staff are always there when I need help.

I continued my treatment with Joan and Peter, improving quickly.

I think my only problem was my speech, which was most embarrassing, having to repeat myself. Then Peter and Joan found a treatment for my speech. I was so excited.

They tested my hearing and found I hadn't been able to listen properly, having a different sound in one ear to the other. This has been the cause of my speech defect. I started the treatment, using headphones and tapes which sent different sounds to each ear. It worked – it's a miracle!

My treatment in Chester is finished now. I don't get embarrassed when I speak or by not doing physical tasks quite as well as the able-bodied, but I am still improving.

The hurdles I overcame in the five years I was at Chester are quite unbelievable. I find myself helping others less fortunate than me. I never thought I would have a future, but my friends in the home come to me for help and advice.

I am asked many times to speak on my disability at meetings and my role in life now seems to be helping and making other disabled people happy.

I am content, happy and look forward to my future. I will always be grateful to Joan and Peter in Chester and my dear Mum and Dad for all their hard work and loving care.

Chapter One

I am a Northerner by birth and although I have spent a large part of my life in the South of England, now I am happy to be back in the North again.

My parents are both from the north, my mother was born in Colne, Lancashire. When she was five years old she moved with the family to Tebay in Cumbria. Her father was an engine driver on the London-Midland-Scottish Railway, when they closed the engine sheds down in Colne he was transferred to Tebay, which is a small village about twelve miles north of Kendal.

Mum attended the village school with her brother and sister. At eleven she passed her exams and gained a place at Kendal Girls' Grammar School. At sixteen she passed the certificate and wanted to go to college to become a teacher but her father told her that Frank, her older brother, was at college and they could not afford for them both to go. So mum decided to train to be a nurse. After writing to many hospitals she was accepted at Keighley Victoria Hospital in West Yorkshire.

Mum told me that the family did not like living in Tebay, it was out in the wilds with only about five shops, no cinema and a poor bus service into Kendal, the nearest town. She says it was a hard time, getting up very early to help her mother before going to school, then again in the evening when she got home. Being the eldest girl she was told it was her duty, she did not mind, but it left very little time for herself or friends, in fact, this was one of the reasons why she went away nursing, to make a life of her own.

My father was born in Bingley a town in West Yorkshire. His father and two sisters all worked in the textile industry. Being the youngest in the family he was spoilt by his two sisters. They told me when he started school he did not like it and would run away at play time, so one of them had to keep an eye on him. He did not want to work in the mills and passed his exams and went to Technical College, then began a five-year apprenticeship as a joiner/cabinet maker.

He told me that he had a very good childhood with plenty of friends who spent most of their time getting up to mischief of one kind or another, but, he says, not vandalism like today! Unlike where mum lived, Bingley had many shops, two cinemas, a theatre, swimming baths and two lovely parks with the river and canal running through.

The family went to Morecambe every year for the annual holiday when the mills closed down for the week at the end of July. Phyllis, the eldest sister, told me one time they were all stood on the seafront watching the tide come in, Doris was standing on the rail to see better, and he pushed her over into the sea. Their Dad and another man had to jump in and pull her out. He said he was only playing and did not mean to push her over, she just lost her balance, but he was always playing naughty tricks or teasing them.

My parents met in hospital, Dad had an accident at work when he was nineteen, injuring his left hand, he had to go to hospital and have surgery. He was then admitted, for a week, to the ward where Mum was working. When he was discharged he asked Mum if she would like to go out with him, and that was the start of their life together.

When Dad was twenty his mother died, she had been rushed into hospital one Monday evening with severe stomach pains. It was found to be cancer which had spread through her body and there was nothing the doctors could do, she died the following Sunday morning. This was a very sad time for all the family.

After Dad had finished his five-year apprenticeship, at the age of twenty-one, he was called up for National Service in the Royal Signals Regiment, where he trained as a wireless operator. After this training he was posted overseas to Egypt, it was the time of the Suez crisis there, so Mum and Dad decided to become engaged while he was home on embarkation leave. It was quite a traumatic two years for every one, not knowing what would happen, but he came home safe and sound, saying it had been a wonderful experience for him.

Mum passed her finals and worked as a Staff Nurse for a while, she then applied for a Sister's post at St. Luke's Hospital, Bradford and was successful. On coming out of the army, Dad went back to his old firm and they began to talk about getting married, but there was a problem. Mum's family were Catholics and Dad's Methodists, they wanted a church wedding and to be of the same religion, so Dad took instruction in the Catholic faith and after six months was received into the church.

This is one story they told me: Dad had always been a very keen cyclist spending many happy hours, and holidays, with his friends cycling together all over the country; the Yorkshire Dales, Lake District, into Scotland, North Wales, Somerset and Devon. He tried to get Mum to go with them, she was not so keen but he managed to persuade her to give it a try. They were out for a ride and Mum took a wrong turn and got lost, Dad had to go back looking for her. He told her, "when we are married I am going to buy a tandem then I will always know where you are", and he did. Mum got her revenge though, Dad had to learn ballroom dancing as that was Mum's favourite hobby.

They started looking for a house and found an old Victorian one overlooking a park in Keighley. It was in good condition apart from the inside decorations, but with help from family and friends, working hard, they cleaned and decorated it throughout, ready for their wedding. They were married on Easter Monday. Mum told me that it was a beautiful sunny day, she wore a long white dress and carried yellow roses, with four bridesmaids all dressed in blue. The church was full, with flowers everywhere, and it was a very moving service. They were blessed, and then they moved up to the high altar, kneeling while the priest continued with Benediction which was very special for them. After a reception lunch at a hotel they went to Southport for their honeymoon.

They had been married nine years, but there was no sign of any children. Both of them wanted a family and they made enquiries about adoption. One morning Mum was at work when the matron called her to her office telling her she had just received a phone call saying Mum's mother had died suddenly.

Mum told me that the death of her mother came as a great shock to everyone. Her father, who had been working the late 10.00 p.m.-6.00 a.m. shift, came home and found her dead in the armchair with a cup of tea in her hand. She'd had a heart attack and must have died instantly. Mum, who was especially close to her mother, took it very badly, she became so ill she was off work for about three months. Dad said that Mum and her mother had a very special relationship with each other.

Chapter Two

About six months after Mum went back to work, she found that she was pregnant, they were both delighted with the news. The only sad thing being that her mother would not be around to see me, she had always said to my Mum: "Don't worry Audrey, it will happen one day and I shall be so proud of you both."

It was a difficult time for Mum during my birth. She was in labour for two days, and in the end they had to send for a surgeon and she had a Caesarean section. Mum knew there was something wrong with me as soon as she held me in her arms. I was as stiff as a board, but the doctor told her, "you have a perfectly healthy baby don't worry yourself". She had to stay in hospital two weeks but she had lots of visitors with family and friends. They all remarked about my hair, or lack of it. Grandad called me 'Baldy', it was a huge joke.

As soon as Mum was back home she asked our own GP to tell her the truth about my birth. He told her, as it was late Saturday night, it took a long time to find a surgeon.

"I think there could be some brain damage due to lack of oxygen at birth," he said. "Wait until she is three months old then I will send you to a paediatrician."

Our parish priest came to see Mum a week later to talk about my baptism. As it was so near Christmas, it was arranged for the following Sunday afternoon. Mum's brother and sister and her best friend, Eileen, were my godparents, there was quite a lot there, with both families and many friends present. I wore Mum's white christening gown which her mother had passed on to her. The service was at St. Joseph's Church, Keighley, then everyone came back to our house for tea. It was a good job we had a large house for them all. Apparently I was as good as gold all day, then screamed for eight solid hours at night. Mum said, "I thought baptism would make her peaceful, so what has happened to Ann?" It's been a joke ever since, and they never tire of telling me.

Early in March our doctor arranged an appointment with a specialist in Keighley, a Mr Roberts. Mum and Dad have told me what he said. He took one look at me then said, "I don't need to examine this baby I can tell she has brain damage. My advice is to put her into a home, she will never walk or talk and just be a cabbage, forget about her and have another child."

Mum was heartbroken, Dad said he just picked me up and walked out of the clinic with Mum crying by his side. My father was so disgusted he wrote to the hospital management to complain, then saw our own doctor and told him what had happened. He was very good and told Dad he knew a paediatrician in Leeds and would write to him to see if he would see us.

We received an appointment to see a Doctor Allibone at Leeds Hospital. As soon as we went into the clinic you could feel a relaxed atmosphere. A lovely Sister undressed me then we went into the consulting room. Doctor Allibone was a small grey haired man with a quiet gentle voice. The first thing he said was, "what a beautiful baby you have, please may I examine her?" When he had finished he said, "I will be honest with you, your child has some brain damage due to lack of oxygen during birth. The good thing is, it is only affecting certain parts of her body and she is not mentally brain damaged."

He was very positive saying, "Ann will need constant physiotherapy and exercise to loosen her body, it will be hard work for you all", but he assured my parents, in time, I would be able to walk and talk, in fact live normally, but at a lot slower pace. My Dad thanked him, saying he would organise the therapy for me and although they were devastated, they were determined to do all they could to help me.

But again my parents came up against another problem, when they inquired at Keighley Hospital about physiotherapy for me, it was refused, because my parents had made a complaint to the hospital. We were told I could not attend any clinics for my treatment at all. My father was so annoyed he contacted Doctor Allibone in Leeds telling him what had happened. Straightaway he said, "if you are prepared to travel, I can organise Ann's treatment here at the hospital." So that is what we did, Mum used to take me three mornings a week, then we would see Doctor Allibone every six months.

This was how we spent the first four years of my life. It was very hard work for Mum, as soon as Dad had left for work, she would feed and dress me, then rush down to the station to get the train to Leeds. Then push me up to the hospital for my treatment, the physiotherapists worked hard with me and showed mum some exercises she could do at home. I loved it, Mum said, I really enjoyed travelling on the train and was always laughing. All the physios called me, "Little Annie, their star".

We then had to do the return journey home. As soon as we arrived back, Mum made me my dinner then put me to bed because I was tired out. When I look back over the years at all the very hard work my dear Mum has done for me, I do not know how she kept going, some days she looked so worn out. I certainly know it is because of all her hard work that I am the person I am now.

My early memories living in Park Avenue are of the large rooms and looking out of my bedroom window at the trees lining both sides of the wide avenue leading to the park gates where Mum took me when it was fine. I have always been fond of trees, Mum says I used to lie in my pram with a smile on my face, watching them with their leaves waving about. I always had my favourite toy with me, a yellow teddy bear, I took it everywhere and would rub it against my face, it was so soft and furry.

My Dad's father remarried two years after his wife had died, and they moved into a flat in Bingley. Phyllis and Doris, his two sisters who never married, stayed in the family home. My Dad helped them modernise it, fitting new windows and doors and decorating for them. Every Saturday morning they would come to help Mum in the house and take me out to give her a break.

Auntie Phyllis was beautiful, she had blonde hair and her face was covered with freckles, such a kind and gentle person. Doris had dark brown hair, she was of heavier build and strong, many a time she would pick me up and carry me in her arms or lift me high to see things better. They both worked as menders in the textile woollen mill just across the road from where they lived and had left school at fourteen, going straight into the mill where their father worked.

They tried to explain the work to me, saying it was looking over the cloth after it has been woven 'mostly suitings' to make sure there were no faults, if there were, they would mend them. About twenty ladies worked in a large room, the cloth was pulled across big tables as they looked for faults. Phyllis told me that it was hard work in the war years. Starting at 6.30 a.m. in the morning until 5.30 p.m. with only fifteen minutes for lunch, and sometimes they had to do fire watch during the night. It was all military uniforms then, Air Force blue was everywhere, but both said some days were very sad when one of the lady's husbands or boyfriend had been killed, or taken prisoner, or they had not had any letters for a long time and were wondering if they were all right.

When I was a little older, about three I think, they asked Mum if I could stay at their house for the weekend. I was so excited, Mum agreed because she knew they both loved me very much and wanted to help her as much as they could. I would be all ready with my little case packed waiting on Saturday morning. If the weather was nice we would take a picnic into Cliffe Castle in Keighley or go on the train to Morecambe. We would play on the sands or have a donkey ride, which I loved. Auntie Doris always made me put a sun hat on but it never seemed to stay on long.

It was such fun being with them, sometimes a little girl called Ruth would come with them, she was the same age as me and we became good friends. Auntie Phyllis was a very good cook and while she was making our meals, Doris would bathe me. She would scrub my neck and clean my ears out, there would be as much water on the floor as in the bath, but we would both laugh. Phyllis would call upstairs to see what was going on.

My auntie's had lovely voices and both sang in the Chapel choir, Phyllis was a contralto and Doris a soprano, they were also Sunday school teachers. Doris had a beautiful voice and sang solo with different choirs, all over the area. People said she could have been a professional, but she was happy just as she was. The house was always full of music, they were in the Bingley Amateur Operatic Society and the Gilbert and Sullivan Society, which put on shows every year and they would rehearse at home. I think that is where I get my love of music from, when I play tapes or go to see a show I think of them often.

Sunday was a busy day, we went to chapel in the morning, we looked smart wearing our best clothes. Phyllis would go straight home after chapel to make the lunch as she was a very good cook and baker. Doris took me with her as she went collecting the holiday club money, she talked so much that we had to run.

We would call at about ten houses, some asked us in for coffee, others gave me sweets or chocolate to eat, we were always late home for lunch. Phyllis would ask what we had been doing, saying all the time, lunch would be spoilt.

In the afternoon we took Ruth to Sunday school with us. I made a lot of new friends and sometimes we would all come back home to play together. We would play in the sand pit in the back garden, or, if it was wet, we would play games inside. When I look back they were very happy times, we would have Sunday school trips to the seaside or into the country, Ruth always came with us and we had lots of fun. I did not want to go home when Mum and Dad came for me, they used to say my aunties spoilt me, but they enjoyed having me and it gave Mum a break.

Chapter Three

When I look back to those happy weekends I think of all the different places my aunties took me to. I enjoyed the outings more so because we took Ruth with us. Bingley is a very pretty town surrounded by hills and there are many interesting things to see.

One of our favourite walks was along the tow path of the Leeds-Liverpool canal from Bingley to Saltaire. On the canal you can see the long narrow barges, these are all used as pleasure boats and are beautifully decorated in bright colours.

In the old days they were the main mode of transport for coal and wool on the waterways of England. As you walk along you pass a number of locks, these are like giant stairways and are a means of raising the boats from one level to another. One of the locks is named the Five Rise Locks, this is a series of five locks, one on top of the other. They raise the water over seventy feet, it's an amazing sight to see the boats go through. I can remember Prince Philip coming to see the lock after it had been renovated, it is the largest one in England.

As you continue the walk you come to another pretty village, Saltaire. It gets its name from a man called Titus Salt. He owned a large textile mill there and built houses, shops, a hospital and a church for all his mill workers. From here you can ride on the small tramway up through the woods to Shipley Glen. This is very popular with children, it has a small fairground with roundabouts, swing boats and arial glide. There are little tearooms and picnic areas where we used to have tea, then we walked back over Baildon Moor and down into Bingley.

Another favourite walk was through Bingley Park along a rough path to Beckfoot which is one of the oldest parts of Bingley. The old stone bridge still stands and you can walk through the ford across the river then up a winding pathway to St. Ives. As you enter the driveway you are met by hundreds of beautiful pink and mauve rhododendrons on each side of the road leading to the Mansion house. This is a huge building, inside there are museum pieces and many valuable paintings. There is a huge dining room, always set up with beautiful china and silver cutlery. Many people go to stay for golfing holidays and they hold banquets there too.

Around this time a lady called Miss Smith who had just retired from nursing asked Mum if she could help with me. My Dad had made the attic into a playroom for me with a carpet on the floor because I used to crawl around as I could not walk. He had made me a large box to stand in with a tray at the front so I could play with my toys or Plasticene, he also built parallel bars to teach me to walk. Miss Smith would come on the mornings I did not go to Leeds for my physio and take me up, we would play with my dolls, dressing and undressing them, and play school. Then she would get my picture books out and read to me, showing me the pictures and explaining what they were, she had lots of patience and helped me a lot, she was so kind.

Later that year Mum's father, Grandad Bob, retired and moved into a flat near where we lived. He would come up to our house in the afternoons and take me out for a walk, or, if it was wet, down to his flat. He was a big believer in fresh air and we would walk for miles, I loved going with him because he would talk and sing to me. Telling me stories about Grandma and Mum when she was a little girl, he always made me laugh. He told me, "Ann you would have loved my Mary Ellen, she was such a kind and jolly person, but she would have spoilt you."

He was a religious man and he would sing hymns and tell me stories of Jesus, he made them so very interesting. St. Anne's Church in Keighley was always open in those days, he would carry me in to show me the altar and the different statues, explaining who they were and what to pray for.

When I look back this was the basis of my faith, which has always played a big part in my life. One incident which I always remember, it was a very hot day Bob had bought us both an ice cream and it was melting fast. As we were near St. Anne's he took me in, we sat at the back eating them when the canon came in and caught us. Granddad said, "this is the coolest place today Father." The canon just laughed and sat with us for a while talking.

We would have tea with Mum and Dad then sit on the settee in the front room and he would read to me. My favourite books were Teddy Bear Annual and Twinkle. In it were stories about two children, Annie and John. He read them so many times we both knew them off by heart.

One day when Miss Smith came she was very upset, and told Mum she would be moving away, her sister was very ill and wanted her to go and live with her in Norfolk. We were sorry she was leaving we had become good friends.

Another change was when Eric, who had the greengrocer's shop, told us he was moving. He lived in a lovely bungalow higher up the road and Mum and Dad had a talk with him and decided to buy it. They had bought this family house hoping to have a big family to fill it, but that would not happen now, as mum could not have any more children, so it was decided we would move.

We loved the bungalow, it had two large bedrooms, a dining room and lounge with colourful gardens back and front. I had the front bedroom with twin beds in it, one for me to sleep in and one for all my dolls, it was so much easier for me to get around being on one level.

Not long after we had moved to the bungalow our Health Visitor called to see us. She told us about a new Children's Clinic which had opened in Keighley, they had a speech and physiotherapy unit as well as all the usual clinics. Mr Skinner was the physio in charge and she made enquires to see if it would be possible for me to attend there instead of making all the journeys into Leeds. She knew all about our problems at Victoria Hospital, and tried herself to get me treatment there but failed. Mr Skinner was disgusted at the way we had been treated, and was prepared to have me there, as it was being run by the local doctors, not the hospital.

My mum phoned for an appointment for me and we went the following week. Mr Skinner was a big, red faced man who lived on a farm in Eldwick. He looked like a typical farmer with big hands and a healthy complexion. After asking mum a few questions he did some exercises with me, very similar to what I had done in

Leeds, then said we could attend twice a week to see how things progressed. The speech therapy unit was very busy but managed to fit me in for one session a week. This would make life a lot easier for Mum, no more train journeys to Leeds for my treatment.

I had one minor set back, with my teeth, which began to crumble. The dentist said it was with all the medication I have been on since birth. He sent me to the Dental Hospital in Leeds and after an examination it was decided the only thing to do was to remove them all and make me dentures. They were so tiny and I had so many problems with them, Mum used to stick them in with Polygrip, which tasted horrible and within the space of two hours they would fall out. It affected my speech and also my eating so we decided to leave them out. I can remember people teasing me and calling me "Gummy", but I took it all in good part.

Our next-door neighbour had a little boy a year younger than me, his name was Gary and he would come round to our house to play. He was very active and never stopped talking but made me laugh a lot. Nearby lived three girls who were a little older than me, Clare, Susan and Alison. They came and asked Mum if they could take me out in my chair to the park, we became good friends and they taught me all kind of things to play.

We had great fun together, my Dad put me a swing in the back garden and they would push me so high. Poor Mum, we nearly gave her a heart attack when she saw me. Alison had two brothers, Mark and Andrew, sometimes they came too and we played school. As Alison was the oldest she was the teacher, she was very bossy and would pretend to give us the cane if we were naughty.

They showed me how to act plays, I had records of Snow White, Cinderella and Sleeping Beauty, we would listen to them then act a play. It was great fun and I learnt a lot from being with them.

One day, Mum and Dad said, "you will be five in December, now is the time to think about school, you should be starting for the January term."

They'd heard of a special school for physically handicapped children in Bradford which was nine miles away. Dad arranged an interview for me and we went one Tuesday afternoon. Of course, dear Grandad Bob came too, he said he must make sure it was the right school for me.

As we drove into the school grounds I could see children playing, some were in wheelchairs, others using walking aids, they all looked happy and seemed to be having lots of fun. I can remember thinking to myself I would love to play with them.

Mr Mitchell, the headmaster, came out to greet us, he was a tall man with black wavy hair and a moustache, he was very jolly and seemed to be full of fun. He took us into his office and told us about his school: 'Lister Lane'. He was very proud of his staff and how much his pupils had achieved with hard work and the dedication of his staff. Pupils were accepted at the age of five to twelve years. We went on a tour around the building which seemed huge, there were ten classrooms, a heated swimming pool and a large physiotherapy area.

He took me to the nursery class, explaining that there were only eight children in every class so they could have individual attention if needed. I met Mrs Dean, my teacher, and her classroom assistant, they were both friendly and said that they would look forward to having me in their class. Then we went to meet Mrs Hobson who was going to be my physiotherapist. I was accepted and was told I could start school in the January term and a bus would collect me at 8 o'clock from home.

I came away very excited, but four months seemed a long time to wait. Mr Mitchell told me there was another boy from our area starting at the same time. He gave us his address and Mum took me to visit him. Granddad Bob said, "Ann, Mr Mitchell is a very kind and dedicated man, there is a lovely atmosphere everywhere in the school, I am sure it is the right place for you."

It was lovely to meet Andrew, the boy who was starting school with me. He was a small built boy with fair hair and blue eyes, he looked just like his mum. I remembered seeing them when I was in the park with Grandad, he was sat in a chair with a long table in front of him painting pictures, I sat with him and we talked about school. He didn't want to go but his Mum, Hilary, said, "You and Ann will go on the same bus together and you are in the same class. It will be nice for you to have Ann as a friend." This made him a bit happier. My Mum and Andrew's chatted about school uniforms and our disabilities. We were different, Andrew wasn't as strong as me, but he could use his hands much better than mine, my hands would never go where I wanted them to go, and I couldn't hold a pencil. Both our families became good friends, we would go out together and to each other's houses. To this day, even though our paths have gone different ways, we remain very good friends.

Over the next few weeks Mum took me into Bradford shopping, there was a large store that sold all different kinds of school uniforms. Lister Lane colours were royal blue, grey and white. I bought a royal blue blazer and sweater, grey pinafore dress, white blouses and knee socks. Then we had to buy shorts for physiotherapy and jodhpurs for horse riding. I chose a brightly coloured duffel bag to carry the things I would need for school.

I was so looking forward to starting, every day I would ask Mum what I would be doing. (I think she was glad when the day arrived). We met Andrew and his Mum a few times, every time school was mentioned he began to cry. He just wanted to stay at home with his Mum.

As it got nearer to my fifth birthday Auntie Phyllis and Doris asked Mum if I could have a big party and invite my Sunday school friends? They told Mum they would do all the work and organise everything. Mum of course agreed so it was arranged for the Saturday nearest the date. My Dad was home and decorated the lounge with streamers and balloons, then fastened all my birthday cards on the wall.

My aunties arrived, loaded with things, and eight of my Sunday school friends came, I had also invited my friends from Keighley, I think there were about sixteen children altogether. Grandad Bob came bringing a beautiful cake, he had asked the bread shop to make it for me. There were sandwiches, sausage rolls, fancy buns and tarts and mum had made a massive trifle with cream and coloured bits on top, everything looked delicious.

Auntie Doris had prepared all the games, she was very good like that, and we had a marvellous party, in no time at all it was seven o'clock and time for them to go home. I thanked everyone for coming, especially my aunties, then Mum gave them all a bag with some cake and goodies to take home. I was tired but it had been a wonderful day, as Mum got me ready for bed I said, "I am five now and can go to school", she just hugged me and laughed saying, "you are funny Ann."

Chapter Four

Early in the New Year we had a heavy snowfall, I kept asking Dad if I would be able to get to school, I did not want to miss my first day. The snow did go and I woke early for my first day at school feeling very apprehensive and wanting to get dressed, but Mum made me have a shower and eat my breakfast first. I felt very grown up in my new uniform and kept looking at myself in the mirror, the time seemed to go so slowly as we waited for the bus to come. Then we heard a horn blow and a knock on the door, when Mum opened it, a nice young lady introduced herself, "I am Mrs Wood, the escort on the bus and Steve is our driver." Mum and Dad gave me a big hug and a kiss telling me to have a nice day, saying they would be thinking about me and looking forward to seeing me at teatime.

There were three children already on the bus, then we went to collect Andrew, he was not ready. His Mum explained she'd had a terrible time trying to get him ready because he was crying all the time, he did not want to go to school. Steve sat him on the seat with me and I calmed him down telling him I would be with him all day.

First we went to Oakworth to collect Graham and continued around Oxenhope, Denholme and down into Bradford collecting children for 'Lister Lane' and the Deaf School. There were twenty-two children altogether, it was a happy journey. Steve was a jolly man, full of fun, and his jokes made us laugh. I remember him saying, "Would you like to go to Blackpool instead of school?" We all shouted, "Yes please".

At last we arrived at school and as we turned into the grounds I could see other buses and the helpers unloading children and their wheelchairs, then it was our turn. I remember having butterflies in my tummy. We were all taken into the hall where waiting to greet us was Mr Mitchell and his staff. He welcomed the old pupils back and then he read the names of the new ones and asked the older pupils to show us around and help us settle in. We said prayers together and then we were taken to our classrooms.

Mrs Dean, who would be my teacher for the first year, took me aside and said, "You will soon find your way around and settle in." I was introduced to Claire, her classroom assistant, then Mrs Dean read out our names; mine was the last, being Whitaker.

I was introduced to Debbie and Jill and they were told to take me into the play area until break time. The three of us hit it off straight away, Jill was a small built girl with long blond hair and walked with sticks, Debbie had brown hair and she was in a wheelchair, she was always smiling.

In the play area there was all kinds of toys and a big doll's house. It had a front on so you could see all the rooms with furniture in them, there was even a bathroom and kitchen just like our house.

When the bell rang for break time it made me jump. Claire, our helper, brought in a crate of tiny milk bottles, I had never seen such small ones. We had our milk and biscuits and then Mrs Hobson, the physiotherapist, came and asked if she could take me down to the therapy department to do my assessment.

She laid me on an exercise mat asking me questions about my mobility and checking my body movements. I told her I had had exercises from an early age and she said she would continue them every Monday and Thursday and take me swimming on Tuesdays. When it was Spring I would be able to go horse riding as they had no indoor facilities for the winter months. In no time at all the dinner bell rang and the kitchen staff brought the food trolley in and we had our dinner in the classroom. Mrs Dean and Claire helped anyone who couldn't manage on their own.

In the afternoon we all gathered around and watched children's television and afterwards Mrs Dean read us a story. At three o'clock the first bell went for the nursery and the youngest children to get ready for home, the older ones went at three thirty. As we got on the bus Steve asked us if we had had a nice day and we set off for home collecting children from the Deaf School then making our way to Keighley.

Mum and Grandad Bob were waiting for me at the door, they couldn't wait to hear all my news about school. I told them about having fun on the bus, meeting Jill and Debbie and my physiotherapy programme. They saw how happy I was, I couldn't eat my tea for talking. I asked Mum to put my bathing costume in my bag as I was going swimming next morning, she was concerned as it always made me tired but I explained Mrs Dean lets us have half and hours rest after lunch.

Granddad Bob was happy for me, especially because I had made friends with Jill and Debbie. Mum asked me about Andrew, I said, "Poor boy, he looked so sad and all he could say was, "home to mum". He did not settle at all in class, he was disruptive knocking all his toys on the floor, spilling his milk and would not eat his dinner. When Mrs Heseltine came to take him for his physiotherapy session he screamed and kicked all the way down the corridor.

After two weeks at school, Andrew started having days off saying he was ill, he just wanted to stay at home. I remember I felt tired one morning and asked Mum if I could stay home for the day, I didn't get away with it though, she said, "there is nothing wrong with you. School for you young lady." I cried but it didn't make any difference, she picked me up and carried me on to the bus still crying, but it taught me a lesson, I never asked again. To this day we still laugh about it.

I continued to spend my weekends with my aunties in Bingley. They couldn't believe how much I have improved since starting school. They enjoyed listening to me talking about my days there, they asked me if I had made any friends and I told them about Jill and Debbie and also about the deaf children on the bus and all the fun we had.

Spring came and Mrs Hobson told me I would be starting horse riding after Easter in Silsden which was near my home.

We went one Thursday afternoon and Andrew, Graham and David came with me. There were four helpers waiting for us and we were soon on horses ready for our first lesson. When we arrived back at the stable my dad was waiting to take Andrew and me home. The lady in charge told my Dad; "This is excellent therapy for Ann, look how straight her back is, it will help with the co-ordination of all her muscles."

I loved sitting on the horse and feeling so tall. When we got home

Dad told Mum what the lady had said. "We will have to find somewhere local for Ann, so I can take her on a Saturday," he added.

Our milkman came from Oakworth and told us he knew a farmer who kept shire horses and his daughter had two ponies. Dad got in touch with him and he told him to take me up on Saturday morning.

We met both Gillian and her Dad. Gillian explained that she did give riding lessons, but had never had anyone disabled before, but she was willing to give it a try. She took us into the paddock and introduced me to 'Pall', explaining he was a very placid, gentle pony. He had no saddle on, just a halter and reins. Pall was a golden brown, with a lovely light brown mane and white dash on his nose.

Gillian told us she did not use a saddle to begin with, it let the rider feel the movement of the horse as it walked along. Dad lifted me on to Pall and I held the reins as Gillian led him around the paddock and my dad walked by my side. It was a wonderful feeling, as I sat on Pall I could feel the movement of his body on my legs and it seemed to make me sit up straight and so tall.

After about half an hour Gillian said, "If your dad could stay with you during your lesson I am sure we can manage, you can come at nine o'clock every Saturday, the lessons are for two hours, I know you will enjoy it."

The first few weeks we just stayed in the paddock walking round. Gillian would teach me the commands for the horse like, 'walk on', 'stay' and 'trot on'. I could grip with my knees and hold the reins. Sometimes we would trot, I could feel all the movements through my body. When I got home I was shattered, Mum used to rub my legs with oil, then I would have my dinner and go to bed for a couple of hours sleep.

I loved every minute of my riding, even if it was wet, we went out for half an hour, then we would go into the stable and Gillian would show me how to look after the horses, all the different names for the brushes, combs and tools for cleaning out their shoes. Then we started going on long rides over the hills in Oakworth. We walked for miles some times across Haworth Moor, the views were magnificent, we could see the steam trains coming up the valley from Keighley. Gillian told me all about the history of Haworth and the Bronte family.

One Saturday we arrived for my lesson and there were crowds of people everywhere. Gillian told us they were filming scenes for the film '*The Railway Children*', she said they had been there all week, around Oakworth station and the village. That day they were filming the landslide scene, where the banking slides onto the track. That was part of our favourite walk so we had to stay in the paddock that day. I have the video of the film and often watch it and remember those happy times.

Another experience I loved was to see Les with his Shire horses, he had four, they were called Colonel, Captain, Sergeant and Big Jim. Big Jim was the largest, I could walk right under him. Although he was big he was so gentle with me and he let me sit on him. Les used to enter them for shows and ploughing competitions all over the country. He had won lots of trophies with them. It was so interesting watching him get the horses ready, the harness and brasses shining so brilliantly, with colourful ribbons in their mane and tail. Captain and Sergeant were brothers and Les had them as a team. Both were dark brown with while socks and a white dash on their heads. They looked so powerful and handsome stood side by side in harness.

Chapter Five

At school Mrs Dean told me when I returned after the summer holiday I would be moving into the infants with Miss Finn, the teacher, and Mrs Sutcliffe her helper, but unfortunately Andrew was staying in the nursery class another term to see if he could settle better.

I had a lovely holiday in Blackpool, Auntie Phyllis and Doris came with us, it was warm and sunny all week and we seemed to spend all our time on the beach or going for long walks. At home I had my friends to play with and the time passed so quickly, before we knew it, it was September and school began once more. Steve our driver had changed his mini bus for a coach because there were more children to pick up. Sometimes it was very noisy on the bus and Mrs Wood had to keep walking up and down telling everyone to be quiet.

In the evening after I came home from school Grandad Bob had tea with us, then he took me for a nice long walk. We both enjoyed them, especially in the spring and summer time, as we usually ended our walks in the park and we would sit and watch people playing bowls. It was nice to sit in the warm evening air and chat to everyone. It was here we met an elderly gentleman who had a golden retriever dog called 'Flip'. He would sit by my buggy and let me stroke him and he would rest his head on my knee while the man talked to us. One evening when we met him, his wife was sitting with him, she was a tall friendly lady and a great talker. She told us she and her husband were members of the "Salvation Army" and that she helped run the Sunday school and would I like to go with her to the citadel just down the road from us.

Grandad told her to ask Mum and Dad because I was a Catholic, but I also went to the Methodist church, he told her where we lived and she called to see us one day. Mum and Dad were happy to let me go as they always encouraged me to mix and to go out and about in the outside world.

I would go to morning mass at St. Joseph's, dash home and have my lunch, then Mrs Sale called for me and walked me down to Sunday school. She looked very smart in her navy and red uniform and little hat, or bonnet, as she called it. When we arrived I was met by Daisy, the junior teacher, and introduced to the other children. We started by singing *'Jesus Wants Me For A Sunbeam'* and we did all the actions to it. Afterwards Mrs Pickles, the Captain, came to say a prayer with us and gave a reading then took us all into the main hall to join the other Salvationists to sing with them and the band. I enjoyed it so much, everyone welcomed me and, although I couldn't sing, I loved the happy rousing hymns they sang. They invited me to join them so I continued going.

Mrs Sale ran the guides every Wednesday night and she asked me to go with her. Mum said if I liked it she would buy me a proper uniform. So I went a couple of times then told mum I wanted a guide uniform, when I tried it on I felt so smart and grown up. I learnt a lot, being with the guides, we had our own little band and I played the tambourine, not very well, but it was nice to be part of it. Some evenings we would learn all the different kinds of knots and then practice tying them. We would split into two teams and play team games and end up singing rounds, which were fun because we would race to see who would finish first. In summer we went for walks and Mrs Sale would point out all the different birds and flowers, we learnt about nature and the seasons of the year. Then the most exciting thing was; 'how to build a camp fire' once it was alight we could bake potatoes and sing camp songs like *'Camp fire's burning, get the engine, get the engine'.*

Every Tuesday Mrs Sale went to help at a club for the elderly at the citadel, during the school holidays I would spend the day there. Mum used to say, "Ann, would you rather be with your friends?" But I told her how I enjoyed talking and listening to the old folk, hearing their stories of days gone by and how times had changed, some of the stories were hilarious and so interesting. Some used cane to make baskets and trays, others were doing fine crochet work, or knitting baby clothes and blankets. Afterwards Mrs Sale would take me to her house for tea as a special treat with Mr Sale and Flip who would sit beside me all the time.

I enjoyed being in Miss Finn's class, we had more work to do but also Miss Finn was the music teacher and we had a piano in our room, so in the afternoon we gathered around the piano and sang. We always did a nativity play at Christmas and parents and friends were invited to watch, so we spent a lot of time practising, I always seemed to be an angel. Mum said, "never mind Ann you may be Mary one year", but I never was.

After Miss Finn's class I moved up into the junior school with my new teacher, Mrs Berry and Miss Thompson, our classroom assistant. They were both younger than the other teachers and Mrs Berry made the lessons a lot more interesting and we seemed to have more fun. She also liked organising educational visits and trips, which we looked forward to.

The first trip we had, which I enjoyed very much, was a day out on the Leeds-Liverpool canal on a pleasure barge. Our school mini bus took us to Shipley where we boarded the barge, we then cruised through Saltaire, Bingley and on to Keighley. We took a packed lunch with us which we ate on board, then the boat turned round and we came back. There were children from another school on the barge with us and they had brought some musical instruments with them, so we all sang songs together and had a lovely time. One thing that I noticed about the trip, it was so very quiet and peaceful, and you had time to see the landscape around you, a lot better than being on the busy motorway.

Another outing we all enjoyed was to Hornsea Potteries on the east coast of Yorkshire, again we went in our school mini bus. We had a guided tour of the factory seeing how the items were made, some of us even had a go at making a pot, but no one succeeded, it is a lot harder than it looks. It was very interesting watching the different processes the clay goes through before the pot is fired. I liked watching the ladies hand paint the pots, they were beautiful when finished. One lady told me you need a good steady hand to do this, I said it is no use me having a try then, with my jerky movements.

One of the most fascinating visits was to the new police station that had opened in Bradford, we were one of the first schools to visit there. A police sergeant was our guide and answered all the many questions that we asked him. He explained all the new technology now used in police work, we watched an interview and cross-examination taking place. Then we had a tour of the cells, he even put some of us inside and locked the door, (not a very nice experience), but it gave me an insight into how the police work. The worse part about our trips was, we always had to write an essay the next day about our outings and try and remember what we had seen.

One morning in assembly Mr Mitchell told us that the parents' association was going to help us raise money for new equipment that was needed in the school. One idea put forward was for a sponsored walk, he asked us all to take a sponsor form home and get our family and friends to sponsor us. All the staff would be involved and would give each child a realistic target to aim for. It was going to be on a Saturday, the kitchen staff would make afternoon teas and other stalls would be set up in the hall.

My target was to walk twice around the school grounds with my wheelchair. Mum, Dad, Auntie Phyllis and Doris came, it was a nice warm day and they all took turns to walk with me. All the other children were doing things, some were swimming in the pool, some were on their bikes, everyone worked very hard but they also enjoyed themselves. The day was a huge success and we raised quite a lot of money for the school funds, I think we all achieved are targets and felt pleased with ourselves. Mr Mitchell thanked everyone for coming and being so generous in giving up their spare time to help. I know I was tired at the end and fell asleep in the car on the way home.

I was still having physiotherapy and I had also started speech therapy, which my Mum was pleased about. Andrew still did not like school and kept having days off. I would sit with him in the bus but I could never get him interested in school, all he used to say was 'home with Mum and play'. They had also moved house and had a stairlift put in for Andrew to take him upstairs to his bedroom. I was glad we lived in a bungalow so that I could get anywhere I wanted in the house.

On the second Sunday of April, during Mass, the parish priest told us there would be a meeting in the school on Tuesday evening, he asked all parents with children who were making their first communion in May to attend. On our way home from Mass I asked Dad if I would be able to make mine, with the other children, as I felt I was ready. He said he would go and talk to Father Hinchliffe about it, which he did and was told, as I went to a different school and would miss the instruction and preparation for my First Holy Communion, he would ask Sister Pascal the headteacher to visit me.

Sister Pascal and Sister Maria came the following Tuesday evening. I felt nervous because Sister Pascal always looked so stern, but she put me at ease straightaway. Mum and Dad left me with them and they explained confession and the receiving of Our Lord's body and blood in the sacrament of Holy Communion. Afterwards they told my parents that I had understood and knew enough about the Catholic faith to begin instruction. Sister Maria would come every Tuesday evening to prepare me and I would then be able to make my First Communion with all the other children. I enjoyed the lessons, although it took me a while to fully understand about confession.

This was the beginning of our friendship with the Sisters, even now, though Sister Pascal is retired and living back in Ireland, we still write to each other. We were invited to the convent in Keighley where they lived, it was a big old building set in lovely, well kept grounds away from the main road and it made you feel so at peace as you walked up to the main door.

Mother Superior welcomed us, she was a very small lady with a lovely smile and she spoke so quietly and gently. She invited us in and told us that there were eighteen Sisters living in the convent and they belonged to the order 'The Cross and Passion', which was founded in the eighteen hundreds in France. The nuns were all teachers or nurses and were very highly qualified. She took us into their chapel, which was quite small but beautifully decorated with flowers. We knelt down together and said a prayer and then went into the parlour for afternoon tea. I had met some of the nuns who came to our church and worked at St. Joseph's School with Sister Pascal, the others worked at St. Anne's and Our Lady of Victory in Keighley.

I soon got used to Sister Maria coming every Tuesday and we sat in the front room on our own for instruction. She explained the Sacraments of Confession and Communion and taught me the Ten Commandments and the catechism that Our Lord gave us. Sister Maria was young and full of fun, she always carried a pair of black gloves with her, I would hide them in different places and she would look everywhere for them and pretend to be cross. I knew I was going to miss those Tuesday evenings with her.

At the beginning of May Mum took me shopping for my dress and a veil for the big day which was only a week away. I chose a white frilly dress with three petticoats under it and pearl buttons all down the front. My head-dress and veil were decorated with blue flowers and I had white socks and black patent leather shoes.

My Grandad Bob came on the Sunday, he couldn't believe it was me. The Mass was at two thirty but we had to be in the church hall by two o'clock to make sure everyone knew what to do, I think everyone was very nervous. We all looked so smart, the girls all in white dresses and veils and the boys wore grey shorts and socks, black shoes, white long sleeved shirts and red ties. Father Hinchliffe arrived with the altar boys and he told us not to worry, he would help us through. We then walked in procession behind Father Hinchliffe, four altar boys, and one at the front carrying the big cross.

As we entered the church the organ started playing and the choir and congregation sang the hymn *'Take Our Bread'*, we walked down the centre aisle to the high altar, which was surrounded in yellow and white flowers. The church was full with parents, relations and friends all gathered there to witness our First Holy Communion. At the altar rail Father Hinchliffe gave a short homily about the sacrament of Holy Communion, which we were about to receive for the first time and the commitment we would make to the Catholic faith.

Communion is given in the form of a small white wafer of bread.

It is specially prepared by nuns and is kept in the tabernacle at the rear of the altar because it represents Our Lord's body. It is placed on your tongue and left to dissolve.

Mass began and, being so near the altar, I watched the altar boys as they served the priest. When it was time for communion Sister Pascal told us to kneel at the altar rail. Then the priest came down the altar steps with hosts in the chalice and blessed us all saying, *"This is the Body of Christ."* Then he placed a host on our tongue. When I had received communion I looked up at the large crucifix and thought of Jesus at the Last Supper with his disciples and I felt a strange sensation pass through me.

It was a very moving ceremony and one I will always remember. After Mass we all had our photographs taken with Father Hinchcliffe on the altar steps, one which I will always cherish. Then Mum, Dad and Grandad Bob came across to me, I could see tears in their eyes. They said, "It is a very proud day for us Ann, seeing you here today." Mum and Dad gave me a big hug and told me how well I had done.

We made our way across to St. Joseph's school hall where the teachers and ladies of the Mother's Union had made a special tea for us. There were sandwiches and fancy cakes and of course jelly and ice cream. More photographs were taken and we received a lovely white missal, a keepsake to remind us of this wonderful occasion that had taken place that day.

A few weeks after I had made my first Holy Communion, Grandad Bob came for tea and he seemed quite excited. He had heard that St. Anne's Church was organising a pilgrimage to Lourdes in September. He had talked about Lourdes many times, but I never fully understood why so many people made the journey there. He wanted us to go with him as a special treat and then I could see for myself what it was all about. It was a five-day tour travelling by air, which was quite enough, because it was a tiring pilgrimage.

We decided to go and Grandad was pleased because he said it would help me to come to terms with my disability. I asked him to explain what he meant by this and he said, "you will understand when you have been, but first I will tell you the story of Lourdes."

I sat and listened, he made it sound interesting and put it in simple terms which I could understand.

Lourdes is a Holy Shrine in a valley in the South of France surrounded by the mighty Pyrenees Mountains where thousands of people from every country in the world go to pray and give thanks to Our Lady. He told me how it all began.

One day in 1858 a young, Catholic girl from a very poor family was out gathering firewood. Her name was Bernadette, she was a frail, sickly girl but very kind towards her family. Whilst she was gathering firewood, she heard a strange sound and looking up, she saw a vision of a lady in white. Bernadette was frightened, she ran home but didn't tell anyone what she had seen.

A few days later she saw the vision again and on the third occasion the lady spoke to her; "Do not be afraid, go and tell the priest what you have seen and ask him to build a church here where people can come to pray and drink water from the spring which I have blessed".

No one believed Bernadette, 'what is the lady's name?' asked the priest. She didn't know, so she ran down to the spring and the vision appeared once more. "Do not be afraid," the lady said. Bernadette asked the lady her name and she replied. "Tell the people I am the Immaculate Conception. Go tell the people and priest to build a church here and pray for me."

In time the priest and the people believed her and although it took many years a beautiful Basilica was built, it had three churches built on top of each other. A cave was dug out of the hillside where the spring was and the water ran down into the river. A marble altar was made with a statue of Our Lady of Lourdes above in the cave. Soon pilgrims were coming to the grotto to pray to Our Lady and St. Bernadette. The small town of Lourdes began to grow as more and more people came to visit. Hotels and shops were built and hospitals where the sick could be looked after. Baths were built so people could take the spring waters and a large square with a huge statue of Our Lady in the centre was erected where people could place their flowers and kneel and pray. Recently a huge underground Basilica has been built which seats twenty five thousand people, so in bad weather the services can be held inside instead of in the open air.

After hearing all this I asked Granddad why so many sick and disabled people went to Lourdes? Was it because they were hoping for a miracle to happen and they would be cured?

He said, "No Ann, they go for reassurance and help to find an inner peace through prayer. You, yourself, will find so many people, more disabled than you are, and you will give thanks to Our Lady for the many gifts you have been given."

I had mixed feelings when the time came for our pilgrimage, we met the other people at the railway station and boarded the train for Gatwick airport. It seemed a long journey, I had never been so far before on a train. We had a meal in the dining car which was a new experience for me. It was fascinating to watch the waiters serving meals on a moving train. I asked Mum if they ever spilt any food and if she could do it, she said, "they have lots of experience, if I did it the food would be everywhere."

We arrived at Gatwick airport and then boarded the plane, Mum and I were very nervous as it was our first time flying. The air stewards soon had everyone seated and told us about the flight. I held my breath while we were taking off, then the stewards started bringing food and drinks round for everyone. After about two hours flying the captain came on the loud speakers telling us we are now flying over the Pyrenees Mountains and should be coming into land in half an hour. Just as we were approaching the airport a thunderstorm started, the aeroplane began to shake and everyone was frightened, but we landed safely.

There were coaches waiting to take us to our hotels where we met our guide and were shown to our rooms. We just had time to have a quick wash and change our clothes before we had to go down to the dining room for our evening meal. It seemed strange hearing people speak in different languages, there were groups from Italy, Spain, Germany and Africa as well as English. The waitresses who came to serve the meal were all French but spoke English which was a relief for us. I wondered what we would be eating, Mum said, "just wait and see then eat what you can". Big tureens of home-made soup and fresh bread were brought in, it was delicious, then we had a stew with fresh fruit to follow. We all drank wine with our meal, I was surprised how sweet it tasted.

Afterwards the group leader told us that there was nothing organised for the evening, but if anyone wanted to go to the torchlight procession they should be in Rosary Square by seven thirty. Dad said he would take me for a little walk while Mum unpacked, then we would all have an early night. As I was getting ready for bed I could hear singing, Dad said that will be the torchlight procession and lifted me up so I could see out of the window. There seemed to be hundreds of little lights all around Rosary Square and the grotto, it was a wonderful sight.

We seemed to have only just gone to bed when I heard Mum talking, I opened my eyes and saw she was already dressed, she said, "I thought that I was an early riser but everyone was up well before six." At breakfast we were served with large cups of coffee and warm croissants with jam, Dad told me this is what they call a continental breakfast.

Our group leader then told us the program for the day. Mass would be said at the grotto at nine thirty, he told us to make sure and get there early as it was always packed with pilgrims around the grotto. Then the rest of the morning was free, in the afternoon the blessing of the sick would be at two thirty and the torchlight procession at seven thirty. We left the hotel and followed the crowds of people down to the domain, when we got to St. Joseph's gate I was overwhelmed to see so many people together, many were in their national costumes and speaking in their native language. Dad said, "I am glad you are in your wheelchair Ann, at least people are letting us through to get near to the grotto."

Walking down the avenue you see the big statue of Our Lady in the Rosary Square, behind is the large Basilica standing so magnificent with its tall spire and the loud toll of the bells as they ring out their tunes. There are guides to help you find your way around and they always make sure that the sick and the disabled are at the front for all the services. Just looking up at the statue of Our Lady in the grotto gave me a feeling of inner peace. Six priests were celebrating Mass, we were glad one was English. As I received communion I thought of Bernadette and wondered how she must have felt all those years ago when she saw the vision of Our Lady. I was glad that my Grandad had brought me to Lourdes and I knew that my faith would take a more meaningful role in my life. After Mass we went along the riverside to where the baths were, there were long queues of people waiting to go in, prayers and the rosary were being said in many different languages. Mum told me that she would take me in the baths before our pilgrimage ended to see if it would help me. As you walk past the baths there are large stands full of lighted candles, some are four feet tall, Grandad said that people came down all through the night when it was quiet just to kneel and pray for their private intentions.

We made our way back to the hotel through the shops selling souvenirs and cafes with tables outside on the pavements, there were people enjoying coffee and delicious cream cakes. After our lunch we all went for a rest in our rooms before going to the afternoon service. It started to rain heavy as we were making our way down to the domain for the blessing of the sick, but within ten minutes the sun came out and everything soon dried up.

The guides showed us to our places ready for the service, then they started bringing the very sick and disabled out of the hospital in old fashioned wheelchairs. There must have been over two hundred of them altogether, it brought tears to my eyes. My Grandad looked at me and said, "Ann, you can see now why I wanted you to come and see so many disabled people, much worse than you are." The service began with the bishop walking down each row of pilgrims with the Blessed Sacrament held high and he blessed everyone as he passed by, then he made his way to the altar to begin Mass. At communion the assisting priests went along each row giving out communion as prayers were said for the sick and the disabled, it was a very moving ceremony that I will never forget. On our way back to the hotel, two elderly nuns stopped us and asked me my name, when I said it was Ann they told me that was our Lord's grandmother's name. Then they said you are blessed with a holy name and a beautiful smile and a face which looks so full of peace.

After our evening meal we decided to go to the torchlight procession, we joined the crowds of people making their way down, many were buying candles to carry in the procession. The guides were organizing everyone into lines, there seemed to be thousands of us, some were in groups and carrying banners with their countries name on and in national costume.

The lines stretched all the way down the riverside, well past the grotto. Then the church bell struck eight, we all lit our candles and started to sing the hymn '*Immaculate Mary*'. We walked all along the river bank past the grotto up one side of the avenue and down the other side, round Our Lady's statue into the large square in front of the Basilica, where we gathered to say the rosary together and to sing hymns. It was a wonderful experience for me, one that I will never forget and, one I shall always treasure.

The next morning we all got up early again and after breakfast we made our way to the Basilica for morning Mass. This is a beautiful church with large statues and flowers everywhere. In the centre there is a large altar with choir stalls either side. Six bishops and six priests were celebrating Mass which was sung in Latin. Not only was it a lovely service, it was wonderful to see the congregation being so friendly and helpful to the sick and disabled.

After Mass our group leader had arranged a tour of the old town, and the house where Bernadette was born and lived with her family. The buildings were very old and a lot smaller than I imagined, they lived above the flour mill, where her father worked. It was just two small rooms for her mother, father and the three children. It made me realize that she was just a poor, ordinary girl who was chosen by Our Lady to tell the world about the healing waters of Lourdes, and to be canonized a saint after her death.

Then we went by coach to Bartres and the sheep fold where Bernadette moved to after the apparitions. She lived a simple life in the peace and quiet of the countryside tending the sheep and reflecting on her life before being accepted into the convent.

In the afternoon Mum said she would take me down to the baths, I asked her what they were like because I was feeling quite nervous, she did not know and said we will have to wait and see. There were lots of people waiting when we got there, but one of the guides told Mum to take me to the front. There are two entrances, one for men and one for women and children, as we went in a nurse told Mum to undress me and put on a robe. The baths are like large stone troughs and a nurse holds you at each side and walks you through the water then lays you down and completely submerges you. When they lifted me out I was dry, I could not believe it, and I have never had an explanation for it. All I can think of is that maybe the spring, that never stops running, is supposed to contain healing qualities and that is why so many Christians throughout the world come to Lourdes.

On our way back through the town we stopped and had a coffee and a cream cake at a pavement café. As I looked around I could see the cable cars going across the valley and the funicular railway making its way slowly up the mountain, it certainly is a magnificent sight. In the evening my Dad and Granddad took me for a walk up the hillside on the outskirts of town. As you look down you can see the Basilica and the grotto with the river flowing alongside and the whole domain, then on the other side the large Stations of the Cross. There are fourteen stations and they stand about twelve feet tall and look so commanding as they trace Our Lord's footsteps to Calvary where he was put to death. We sat there a long time just gazing around, each with our own thoughts about this very special place. Then we made our way slowly back to our hotel and another early night.

On our last full day, our leader told us Mass would be at ten o'clock in the underground Basilica, afterwards the rest of the day was our own free time. We could not believe how many people were waiting to go in, Grandad explained the Basilica to me. It is the largest church in Lourdes and can hold over twenty five thousand people, there would be over fifty bishops and priests celebrating Mass. It was a long Mass with so many people taking communion, and I would not have missed it for the world. The priests feel it is an honour to celebrate Mass in the Basilica, and the pilgrims, a privilege to take part. I will never forget it, I felt so emotional when the organ started to play and the long procession of altar boys, bishops and priests made their way to the high altar in the centre of the Basilica.

I must mention one incident on that day, when I woke up my right eye felt sore and would not open. Dad took me to the hospital dispensary where they gave me some ointment to put on to soothe it, but nothing seemed to happen and it still would not open. Grandad was concerned and said that he would take me to the grotto and bathe my eye with the spring water. Within half an hour the soreness had gone and I could open my eye. It was like a little miracle, it certainly made me believe that the spring waters had healing powers.

We went shopping in the afternoon for gifts and souvenirs to take home with us and, like the other pilgrims, we bought special water bottles so we could fill them at the spring then get them blessed and use as holy water at home.

This being our last evening we decided to join in the torchlight procession to give thanks for the inner peace and joy that our pilgrimage had given us. We also collected the photographs that had been taken during the week, these I still have and often look at and remember my first visit to Lourdes.

The day came to return home, most of us felt sad. It had been a tiring five days but everyone agreed that it was well worthwhile. Our group leader had arranged for us to have Mass at the Grotto at eight thirty that morning. Grandad told me not to be sad, he said, "when we get to the grotto Ann, I will show you a special spot on the ground and if you kneel down and kiss it you are sure to return." As I sat in front of the altar and looked at all the pilgrims around me I closed my eyes and prayed for all the people that I'd met, and especially for my dear granddad and my parents for giving me the opportunity to come to this wonderful place - Lourdes. I looked at Our Lady's statue and the statue of Bernadette and I knew I would come back one day.

The coach arrived to take us to the airport, we said our goodbyes to friends we had made in the hotel then got on the coach and off we went. We had a short wait at the airport then it was time to board the plane. As we were going up the steps I turned for a last look around, thanking God for giving me the inner peace which I felt and the strength to carry on and to overcome my disability.

I have been back many times since then, with The Handicapped Trust, Hosanna House and with my parents. One pilgrimage I will always remember is when I went with my Dad and the children and staff of St. Joseph's school. My dear Sister Pascal, St. Maria and Father Hinchcliffe led our group and he made it so very interesting and easy to follow, he was a wonderful priest.

One of the many happy memories of that week was of Sister

Pascal dressing me, we could not stop laughing, then we walked down from the hotel to the domain. She was trying to push my buggy with the brake still on, we ended up with a square wheel! I teased her all week about it and told everyone we had made a hole in the wall.

Each time I have been given strength, but most of all a richer and fuller meaning of my faith, which is so special to me.

Chapter Six

When I returned to school after my holiday in Lourdes, I was moved into Miss Bargette's class. She was a lovely lady with dark brown hair and spectacles, she was always smiling. We all enjoyed her lessons because she made them so interesting, even when it was maths, which I found hard, she would make it into a game so that we could understand what she was trying to teach us.

Every afternoon Miss Bargette would read to the class, my favourite were the 'Katy' books, especially the stories when she was at boarding school. I would go home and tell Mum and Dad about this girl called Katy who had gone away to a girls' boarding school and all the things that the girls got up to. They seemed to have lots of fun in their dormitory at night, with pillow fights and midnight feasts. I asked Mum if I could go to a boarding school? Mum and Dad understood how I felt because the school run was now a lot longer. This meant that I spent a lot more time travelling and less time in school lessons.

Dad said he would have a word with Father Hinchcliffe, our parish priest, and see if he knew of a school for me. Father Hinchcliffe told us that, when he was in the Dewsbury parish, he knew a girl called Mary Hemingway, who was very much like me and he helped to place her at St. Rose's, a boarding school for girls in Stroud near Gloucester. The head teacher was Sister Quentin and Father Hinchcliffe said that he would write to her and tell her about me and see if we could visit the school.

About two weeks later we received a letter from Sister Quentin inviting us to visit St. Rose's on the fifth of December, which was my birthday. Grandad said, "that is a good omen Ann," but I did not know what he meant by that. I was so excited, all that I could talk about was boarding school. Mum kept telling me it was only an interview and they may not be able to take me, she told me not to build my hopes up too high.

The days seemed to drag by, I asked my Dad if he had planned a

40

route out for the journey, he told me that he had, but it was going to be a long drive, about 250 miles. We would need to set off at seven a.m. to get to the school for lunch.

We were all up early that morning, Mum had packed sandwiches and a flask of coffee for the journey and it was just seven a.m. when we set off. The motorways then were not as busy as they are now, and we had a good run down the M6 and onto the M5 for Gloucester. We had a couple of stops at the service stations, and it was just ll.45 a.m. when we arrived at St. Rose's. Sister Quentin came out to meet us and took us into the dining room for lunch, which was very welcome after the long journey.

When we had finished lunch Sister asked some of the girls to take me upstairs and show me the dormitories and the playrooms. Mum and Dad went into Sister's office for coffee. They told her about me and Sister told them about the school. It was a small residential school for girls, with fifty boarders and eight day pupils who lived in the area. There were six Sisters on the staff as well as twelve others. They had a new therapy area and a medical centre.

The bell went for afternoon school and Jacky White took me to Sister's office and she gave us a tour of the school. I wanted Mum to see the dormitories. In the younger children's dorm there were eight beds, with a play area at the large window end, which looked out onto the lawns and garden. I was very excited and could just imagine myself sleeping in one of those beds.

We then all went back to Sister's office and she asked me what I was doing at school and what I liked best. She kept looking at me and then said, "you remind me of a girl we had here a while ago called Mary Hemingway." Dad said, "yes, Father Hinchcliffe mentioned the likeness when I talked to him about a school for Ann." Sister then told us that she had no place for me at the moment, but two of the girls were leaving early next term.

"So we could find a place for you to begin after the Easter holidays for the summer term. That will give you time to arrange everything at home, I will give you a clothing list and what you need to bring with you."

We then had a cup of tea and biscuits and set off on our journey home. It was very dark driving home and Dad took a wrong turn and got lost, so we did not get home until ten o'clock. I had fallen asleep in the back of the car, so Mum just put my pyjamas on and put me straight into bed where I slept for twelve hours.

That weekend I had my birthday party, Auntie Phyllis and Auntie Doris came and brought all my friends from Bingley. Grandad Bob was there and I told them all about our visit to St. Rose's and that I was going away to boarding school next April. I think it came as a shock that it had happened so quickly, but they all agreed that it was the best thing for me. I would be getting full time schooling and all the therapy I needed without the long bus journey each day that I found so tiring. Grandad said, "at least Ann we will know what to buy you for Christmas this year. You will need so many things to take with you. I think we should start and make a list now don't you?"

It was soon Christmas time and I did not know then that it would be the last one for Auntie Phyllis. We had gone to their house on Boxing Day for tea, later Auntie Phyllis asked Mum to go upstairs to her bedroom. She had found a lump under her arm and wanted Mum's advice, Mum told her to go see her doctor as soon as possible and let him advise her. Auntie Phyllis had asked Mum not to say anything about this to anyone, and it came as a shock when she had to go into hospital in January for an operation to remove her breast. We were all very upset when we visited her in hospital, especially Auntie Doris. Phyllis looked so ill, I asked Mum what was wrong, and she told us Auntie Phyllis had cancer, they had removed a breast but unfortunately it had spread into her body and there was no more that they could do for her.

Auntie Phyllis came home for a few weeks and we took her out wherever she wanted to go, to visit her favourite places, but it was not long before she was too ill to travel. She went into a hospice and a few days later she died. We were all so very sad and upset, she was only forty years old and such a lovely person who had never done any harm to anyone all her life, it seemed so unfair. Poor Auntie Doris was heart broken. My Dad said, "I don't know how Doris will cope on her own, she always relied on Phyllis so much, it is going to be hard for her now."

Those next few days were the worst that I had ever known, there seemed to be so much happening, friends and relations calling, the funeral to arrange. My Dad spent a lot of time with Doris organising everything, she did not want to be left on her own at all. I cried so much Grandad Bob said it would be best if he looked after me the day of the funeral. He said it would only upset Doris more, seeing me cry all the time.

That night when Dad put me to bed, he told me about the service. The chapel was packed with all her friends and workmates, the choir sang beautifully and the minister spoke so well about Phyllis and all the good work that she had done, it was a lovely service. Dad said we must remember all the happy times that we had together and not be sad, Phyllis was now in heaven with Jesus and would watch over us always.

I thought things would never be the same again, but Mum told me, "Ann, we all have to keep going. We have to accept the bad times with the good. None of us will ever forget Auntie Phyllis, she played a big part in your life and you have a lot to thank her for. Now we must carry on, that is what she would want us to do, not to be sad all the time."

I think getting ready for boarding school helped me a lot then, we had to buy my school uniform and all my other clothes, as well as everything else that I would need to take with me. We had a big party at Easter with all my friends from Bingley, as well as the ones living near us. The house was packed and everyone said that they would miss me, I told them that I would be home at half term to tell them all about life at boarding school.

At last the day came, Mum had all my clothes ready and marked. Dad packed my case and had to sit on it to fasten it, he then loaded the car and we were ready for off. It was a nice day and we had a good journey down arriving about half past two. Sister Valerie met us and took us up to my dormitory and we unpacked. Mum arranged all my clothes in my wardrobe and my drawers for me, then we had tea and it was time to say our goodbyes. I was a bit sad, and I think Mum and Dad were too, they both gave me a big hug and told me they loved me, then they got in the car and I waved them off. Sister

Valerie took me back up to my dormitory and introduced me to the other girls, I remembered Jacky White from my interview, we soon made friends again and she was my best friend all the time that I was at St. Rose's.

The other girls in the dormitory were, Mary, Amanda, Bernadette and Julie, we soon got to know each other and we all became good friends. Then Sister Valerie called, "we are having early tea today, so everyone down to the dining room please." Jacky said. "just follow me Ann you will soon find your way around." I sat with all the girls from my dormitory and they all told me where they came from and I told them all about myself. Then after tea we went back upstairs to the playroom, Jacky was teasing me about bath time, she said, "watch out for Sister Valerie, she will scrub you all over." Just then Sister called, "bath time for Ann", and it certainly was the bath of my life. She said, "let me look in your ears Ann", also she gave my hair two washes! When I went back into the playroom all the girls said, "did you enjoy your bath Ann?" and started to laugh, but it was all in fun.

At bedtime Sister Quentin came in to say goodnight and to see if I had settled in all right. She told me not to be homesick, and told all the girls to look after me and make me feel at home.

Friday morning came, my first day at boarding school. I was in Mrs Mason's class with my friends from my dormitory. She soon made me feel welcome and at ease. I enjoyed the lessons because she made them interesting and amusing. In the afternoon Miss Thompson, the physiotherapist, came to see me and took me to the therapy department to do my exercises. Gosh she did put me through it, and nicknamed me nosy because at that time I could not keep my head still.

The following Monday was May Day, so we had a long weekend off, as most of the children lived a long way from school they stayed there. It was a good time for me to find my way around and to get to know the other house mothers. Ours was called Felicity, she was young and full of fun and played games with us. As it was quite warm, we were allowed to play outside on the lawn which was good fun. Each dormitory had a name, ours was called St. Albert's and it was nice for me to be in the bed next to Jacky because she helped me so much. At the weekend I could phone home and as my speech was not too good Jacky would help me, we became the best of friends.

Every Wednesday Sister Valerie made the breakfast, it was always beans on toast. We would all say that Sister Valerie could not cook, but we all loved her. She would pretend to be cross with us, and then come round and ask if we wanted extra toast.

During my first term I spent a lot of time, learning to walk with Miss Thompson. I found this so hard and frustrating, but with encouragement from everyone, especially my friends who would shout "COME ON ANN, YOU CAN DO IT", I kept on trying. Miss Thompson said how nice it would be if I could surprise Mum and Dad by walking to meet them on Speech Day in July. I had three months to reach that goal and I made it, only one dozen steps, but the smiles of happiness from my parents, and being on my feet at last, made it all worth while.

It had been a long, hot summer term, but a very happy one. I felt I had grown up quite a lot. We were allowed to watch 'Top of the Pops' every week and I became a big fan of the groups '*Brotherhood of Man*', who won the Eurovision Song Contest with their song '*Save all your kisses for me*', and the '*Bay City Rollers*' singing '*Bye, Bye Baby*'.

It was time to say goodbye to every one and take our summer holiday.

Chapter Seven

After a lovely summer break with my parents, I was looking forward to going back to school and seeing my friends again. Dad was taking me by car to Sheffield and Mrs Mason, our escort, would take me and four other girls who lived up north by train to Gloucester. We had fun on our journey, I was hoping I would still be in St. Albert's dormitory with the same girls.

Sister Quentin was waiting to welcome us back, she introduced us to Sister Teresa who would be taking me for physiotherapy. She gave me a big hug and said, "Oh no, we have another Mary here!"

Our little group was still together in the dormitory, and were to be in the same classroom too. On our first day we were introduced to a new teacher called Mrs Dove who would be taking us for religious instruction. She was a gentle lady who taught us so much and we all grew to love her. Every month, each class took turns to do morning assembly. We acted a little play from a story in the Bible which Mrs Dove rehearsed with us. Life continued to be very happy, both in class and out of school hours, apart from my maths, I enjoyed the lessons. I had continuous physiotherapy which left me exhausted at times, but I was improving physically so it made it all worthwhile.

We used to look forward to the weekends, a lot of the girls were weekly boarders so there weren't many of us left. Every Friday evening a man called Mr Smith brought us films to watch, *Born Free* was my favourite. Saturday afternoon we went into Stroud and were allowed to buy a quarter of sweets. In the evening we watched the television, there were good programmes on, *The Generation Game, Juliet Bravo* and, of course, everyone's favourite *Dallas*. We were allowed to stay up until nine p.m., then Sister Quentin would help us undress for bed.

Sunday was a quiet day starting with Mass in the school hall, then the priest stayed for lunch, we had to be on our best behaviour! Jackie helped me phone my parents in the evening.

Term time passed quickly and in no time at all we were preparing for Christmas. December was my favourite month because we started preparations around the fifth, which was my birthday. We helped the staff to make paper chains and decorate the Christmas tree. There were decorations everywhere in the dormitories.

On the night of my birthday Sister Quentin told us all to go into the playroom and look out of the window. What a lovely surprise, a bus stood outside and it was decorated with Christmas lights and people were singing carols. We were excited about the Christmas services and parties we were having. Sister Valerie tried her best to keep us calm telling us we still had two weeks before school term ended.

Mrs Dove told us the Christmas story and made it into a play which we all took part in for our parents and friends. Then it was time to say goodbye and make our journey home for the Christmas holiday. Dad came to collect me in Sheffield and I couldn't wait to get home to see my dear Mum. She was excited to see me, and the bungalow looked so festive with tree, cards and decorations.

It turned out to be a very hectic but enjoyable three weeks. Dad took me to see my friends in Bingley and Keighley and Mum threw a big Christmas party for all the family. My dear Grandad Bob was with us almost every day. He had missed me but was so happy I could walk, there were tears in his eyes. The biggest surprise of all was when our dear friend Sister Pascal walked in, Mum and Dad hadn't told me, I could hardly contain my excitement. It was great to see her and she was amazed at the progress I had made.

All too soon, it was time to start another term at school. As always, I was sad to leave my Grandad and parents, but I was looking forward to seeing all my friends at school.

We were moved into Blessed Margaret's dormitory, and also into Mrs Dove's class, it was good that Sister Quentin kept us all together. Mum and Dad came down to stay for a weekend in February and told me Grandad Bob was ill. Mum told me not to get too upset, just say my prayers for him. Ash Wednesday was the last week in February, I remember being upset and not being able to settle, I didn't know why. After Mass in our little chapel Sister Quentin and Mrs Dove came to see me, I thought I had done something wrong.

They told me my dear Grandad Bob had died that morning and had gone to heaven. It was a shock and I cried and cried. I loved him so much.

Mrs Dove was a great comfort to me over the next few weeks helping me to come to terms with his death. Mum and Dad came down at the weekend and she told me to be very brave for my Mum's sake. They were a tower of strength to me but they wouldn't let me go to his funeral, instead we had a Mass in our little chapel. It took me a long time to come to terms with losing Grandad, he had taught me all about the Catholic faith and had always been there for me when I needed a friend to talk to.

I enjoyed being in Mrs Dove's class, she was a good teacher and I stayed with her for three years. Her husband was a maths teacher at our school, he was very strict and made us work. None of us were good at maths but Mrs Dove used to help us with the homework he gave us, (thank goodness he never found out).

I had another shock in March, my best friend Jackie was taken into hospital, she had a valve in her brain and it was blocked. She died and I grieved so much for her she was so young, and a loving, caring friend.

When I went home for the Easter holidays, Sister Quentin gave me a letter to give to my parents. She was taking a group of children to Rome in May and wanted their permission for me to go with them. Mum and Dad said that it was an opportunity I must take as it would be a wonderful experience, especially as she had managed to get tickets for an audience with the Pope.

The Pope is the head of the Catholic church and lives in the Vatican in Rome, and we Catholics feel that it is an honour to meet him in person.

I returned to school looking forward to our holiday in Rome, we were going by air from Heathrow airport and staying in a large hotel in the centre of the city. I shared a room with Sister Teresa which I liked because we got on so well together and had lots of fun. Sister Quentin had planned the whole week out so we could visit the important places like the large Basilicas of St. Peter's, St. Paul's and St. John's. We also visited the Coliseum, the Trevi

Fountain and the Spanish Square with the hundred steps. We walked over St. Angel's Bridge into the Castle and the Arch of Constaine. They are all old buildings and although very beautiful, they did not appeal to all the girls, there were too many steps everywhere. The temperature was over one hundred degrees, we were so hot we seemed to stick to our wheelchairs.

Our best day was Wednesday when we had an audience with Pope John Paul in St. Peter's Square. Sister Quentin told us to wear our best dresses and school blazers and to be on our best behaviour! We were all excited and had an early breakfast as we had to be there by nine o'clock even though the Pope did not come out onto the balcony until eleven.

We did not know what to expect, there were thousands of people of all nationalities and denominations. We were fortunate to be on the front row just by the balcony where he stands to address the people and to give them his blessing. When he came out, it was a breathtaking sight, the Holy Father was dressed in red and white vestments. He carried a large crucifix and wore a red and gold mitre on his head. Cardinals, bishops and priests were with him, also his personal Vatican guards in their bright scarlet uniforms. First he gave the congregation his blessing in many different languages before coming down to meet the people.

There was complete silence all around the square even though there were thousands of people. It was a very emotional atmosphere, some were crying, some saying the Rosary. When he came near us to speak, we could see a very kind and gentle face, full of compassion. He shook a hand, touched a face and placed his hand on our heads, then he spoke with sincerity. He asked me if I was English, then he blessed me and placed his hand on my head. We were in St Peter's Square for four hours but it had not seemed so long.

When he had finished his walk about, he went back onto the balcony and gave us all a final blessing before leaving. It was such a wonderful experience and so emotional we all felt at peace with ourselves, I would not have missed it for anything. We all had our photograph taken with him, it is one of my many treasured possessions. It had been an honour to meet him. Just as the audience had finished the heavens opened and there was torrential rain. The local people came over to us with black bin liners to put around us, we did not mind the rain it had been such a wonderful morning.

On our last night we had a party in our hotel after the evening meal and invited the group of French children who were also staying in the hotel. It was great fun trying to understand each other, we could only speak a few words of French, and they did not understand everything we said, but we all enjoyed ourselves, even the staff joined in and had a good laugh.

As I lay in bed that night and looked back over the week, at all the wonderful places we had been to and the many different things that we had done, I was so glad that my parents had given me this opportunity to visit Rome, and what an honour it was for me to have met our Holy Father and receive his personal blessing.

Next morning we had to be up early, have breakfast, and be ready for when the coach came to take us to the airport and our flight back to England. We were all feeling a little sad, then Sister Quentin said, "just look back on this holiday and remember all the beautiful places we have visited and that wonderful morning when we met Pope John Paul and the blessings he gave each one of us". It had been an experience that we would always remember and treasure in our hearts and look back on all our lives.

We had a good flight home and our mini bus was waiting at Heathrow when we arrived back to take us to school. There was lots to talk about on the way until Sister remarked, "don't forget, Mrs Dove wants a full page essay on Monday all about this holiday," that brought us down to earth again.

Chapter Eight

At the end of June we were having our Annual Summer Fete, and this year Sister Quentin had invited some of the old girls down to a reunion and to stay over for the fete. Mum and Dad were coming down for the weekend and bringing Auntie Doris with them. I was looking forward to seeing them and telling them about my holiday in Rome and meeting Pope John Paul.

It was a lovely sunny day and the gardens were all set out with stalls, games and side shows, there was balloons and bunting everywhere and a band was playing. Mum and Dad had stopped for lunch on the way down and arrived at 1.30 p.m. We were walking around looking at the stalls when Sister Teresa called, "Ann, I have someone here who I want you to meet." As we made our way over I could see this young lady with Sister, then she introduced us. "Ann, this is Mary Hemmingway who I have talked to you about." As I looked at Mary I could see the resemblance, not just in appearance, but that she was an Athertoid like me. I stayed with Mary quite a long time and she helped me to understand my disability more, she told me that I had a lot of hard work in front of me but, like Mary, I was determined to make the most of my life.

On the Sunday Dad took us all to Gloucester for lunch and, in the afternoon, we had a walk around the city centre and the Cathedral. Then we sat in the grounds just talking about my holiday in Rome. Mum, Dad and Auntie Doris were so pleased for me, that I had had the opportunity to meet the Pope. Mum said, "your Grandad Bob would have been so proud if he could see you now and the improvement that you have made this year".

When we arrived back at St. Rose's, Sister Valerie told my parents that Sister Quentin would like a word with them before they went home. We went along to Sister's office and she asked us if we had thought about my future when I would have to leave St. Rose's next year? Sister advised my Dad to get in touch with Bradford Further Education and Careers Office to find out about placements after I was sixteen.

We all had tea together and then it was time to say goodbye to Auntie Doris and my parents. Mum said, "never mind Ann, only a few weeks and then you will be home for the long summer holidays." I did not feel so bad when they had left.

I had a lovely holiday, Dad had three weeks off work so that we could all be together. We went up to the Lake District where Mum re-lived her childhood, she showed me the schools that she went to, the house where she lived from being five years old until she was sixteen, and the walks and the picnics she'd had with her family. It was a lovely little village called Tebay just outside Kendal, the River Lune runs through it and she pointed out where she used to swim with her school friends. It was full of salmon and anglers came from miles around to fish, she used to love to watch the salmon leap out of the river.

My Dad took us on a mystery tour into the Yorkshire Dales. The scenery is breathtaking, you can see for miles over the rolling hills and fields which are divided up by stone walls and all the farm buildings are built with limestone, it looks like a giant jigsaw puzzle. The TV series *'All Creatures Great and Small'* was made around this area and now it is a big tourist attraction.

Another day we went to the village of Esholt, this is called *Emmerdale* in the television soap. We walked around and saw the post office, the church and, of course, the 'Woolpack' pub. It was called the 'Commercial' then but they would hang the Woolpack sign up when they were filming. (It has now changed its name to the Woolpack as in the soap). My Dad knows his way all around as he used to cycle all over in his younger days.

Dad made an appointment to see the careers officer in Bradford to discuss my further education and also what I could do when I left school after I was eighteen. Unfortunately they could not offer me anything at all. Most of the special schools and day centres were for mentally disabled young people. He told Dad that the north of England was not as well equipped as the south, where they seemed to do more for the physically disabled.

So Mum and Dad had a good talk about everything and decided, if there was nothing here for me, then we would have to move down south. They started looking for work and one day Dad was in the library looking through the education news supplement and saw a special college in Hampshire was going co-ed and they were advertising for teachers, nurses and care staff. He wrote off for an application form and details about the college. Mum thought, with her being a nurse, that maybe they could both work there. She said with me being at boarding school we would have the same school holidays and it should work out fine.

After reading the brochure and filling in the application forms they were both invited down for an interview and to look around the college. They could not believe their luck when both of them were offered jobs, Mum as a nurse in the medical centre and Dad as a woodwork teacher and to work in the boy's boarding house. It would be a big change for everyone, to sell our lovely bungalow and move three hundred miles away from family and friends and start a new life in Hampshire. Mum said, "we have to think of Ann's future, she cannot sit at home and do nothing with her life." So they decided to take the opportunity that the college offered them and to move down south, luckily for them there was a flat vacant above the medical centre which they could have so that was one worry less. They would have plenty of time to look around before buying a house. In no time at all things started happening for them, a man came one day and said he had heard that we may be moving. He said his wife and he always looked at our bungalow as they passed on the bus and it was always kept so nice. If we were moving, he would buy the bungalow from us, so that was the biggest thing done with.

My mum said, "Ann, I will pack all your things now ready for school, you will not be coming home here again. We will just have time to see you off and then we will be busy with the move, it is a good job that the college term does not begin until the last week of September, we should just about make it."

When I arrived back at school I found I had been moved into one of the downstairs dormitories, it was called Holy Child and I was in with Patsy, Julie and Angela and we were all still in Mrs Dove's class. We all got on really well together and had lots of fun at night in the dorm. Angela had brought a small radio cassette player back with her and we used to listen to pop music and tapes. Sometimes we were told off by the house mothers for playing the music too loud, then we would put on a talking book tape and all get into bed with the volume turned down and fall asleep.

One day at the end of September I was with the riding group and the instructor told us, in a few weeks time, there was going to be an important visitor coming to the stables. We all wanted to know who it was but she would not tell us, she just said, "I want you all to work very hard during the next two lessons so that we can put on a good show for our V.I.P. I have told your house mothers to make sure you are all neat and tidy with boots polished, and don't forget to bring your riding hats."

When our mini bus arrived at the stables the following week we could not get near and had to be escorted by a police car, there seemed to be police everywhere. We wondered what it was all about, then a limousine arrived with a flag on the front and Princess Anne and her lady-in-waiting got out. Princess Anne is the Patron of 'Riding For The Disabled', and had called to see us on her way to other engagements in Gloucester.

We were all very excited but we also felt honoured that Princess Anne had come to see us. She spent about an hour with us and was very interested in how we managed to ride. Some of the disabled cannot sit astride a horse and have to use a sidesaddle. We were all introduced to her and she talked to everyone, we were a bit on edge, but she soon made us feel relaxed and we were chatting away. She made us laugh when she told us that she fell off her horse the first time that she tried to jump a fence.

It was another special occasion for me to treasure, the other girls at school were very jealous when we told them that we had met Princess Anne at the riding school and wanted to hear everything about her visit.

When half term came Sister Quentin told me that I would be going on the mini bus to Reading with six other girls. We stopped at the Little Chef just off the M4 motorway and our parents collected us from there. I was looking forward to going to our new flat at the college in Hampshire and meeting new friends. Mum and Dad were waiting for me when our mini bus arrived and soon had my case in the boot and we were on our way. Dad said it was about an hour's drive through some lovely countryside. He said, "I think that you will like it down here."

We had a lovely drive, the views were so different from the ones in Yorkshire, the countryside seemed more open and not as rugged. I was amazed how big the college was when we drove in the entrance and saw all the buildings. Dad said it was the largest college for the disabled in the country with 300 students, nearly all of them boarders. It is called Lord Mayor Treloar College and was started by the Lord Mayor of London in 1906 for sick boys, to take them out of the city and into the country, at that time they were mostly TB and polio cases.

The flat we had was quite large with two big bedrooms and the lounge looked out over the grounds, Mum said, "the only trouble is Ann, it is miles out in the country and the bus service is terrible." The nearest town was Alton four miles away where you could buy your weekly groceries but there were no large stores. We had to travel to Guilford or into Winchester, both about twenty five miles away, for clothes and other shopping.

One good point about living at the college, they had a large heated swimming pool so Dad could take me in, any time out of school hours. I enjoyed that, but it seemed strange not seeing students around, it was so quiet everywhere. Before I went back to school Mum told me that Auntie Doris had asked us to spend Christmas with her and to stay at her house. I said, "that would be lovely, we will be able to see all our friends and relations again, and I can tell them about our new home."

It was a very busy time when I got back to school Mrs Dove was putting on a special show for Christmas, and we seemed to spend every spare moment rehearsing, she even came in on a Saturday morning! The housemothers were busy making our costumes and props for the show, and as the time got near, everyone was so excited, learning their lines and trying on their costumes.

The show was like a pantomime with all the younger children dressed as different animals and the older ones dressed as characters from nursery rhymes. We put the show on both Friday and Saturday and everyone who came said that they had enjoyed it. We had all been so busy the weeks seemed to fly by and when my birthday came Mum and Dad could not get through to see me as they were both busy at the college. I did not mind because I knew that I would see them at Christmas. As we were getting ready for our Christmas party in our dormitory, Patsy said, "do you realise this is the last time we will be together for Christmas?"

"I wonder where we will all be next year, when we have left school?" said Angela. We were all quiet for a while and then I said, "well, let us make this party the best one we have had at St. Rose's." It certainly was, after the Christmas meal, which was excellent, we all moved into the hall and put records on and danced and played games until eleven o'clock. The staff then helped the housemothers to put us all to bed.

Next day we packed and I went on the mini bus to Reading where my Dad was waiting for me. He said Mum was busy getting everything ready for Bingley as we were spending Christmas and the New Year with Auntie Doris so there was quite a lot for Mum to do.

When we arrived home Mum had a lovely meal ready for us, which we all enjoyed, she said it was no use decorating the flat, as we would be away most of the holiday. Next day we went shopping into Winchester, there was a large Christmas tree all decorated with lights and the shops looked lovely with fairy lights and fancy decorations everywhere. We did our shopping, buying presents for family and friends in Yorkshire, we did not buy any food to take with us, my Dad said we had better see what Doris has bought in first. I helped Mum pack in the morning then we cleaned the flat in the afternoon and had an early night, Dad wanted to be off early next morning for the long journey north.

We had a good run, the roads were not too busy and there were no hold ups on the motorway. We stopped to stretch our legs and for refreshments, it took us six hours to get to Bingley. Auntie Doris was pleased to see us but her house was in a mess, the curtains were down and furniture piled in the centre of the room. She said she had a meal in the oven but she had not finished all her cleaning yet, so Dad put the clean curtains up and Mum helped to finish the cleaning, then we sat down to a lovely meal and a good chat. Dad said he would take Doris shopping next day while Mum and I put up the tree, then we would all help with the decorations.

It seemed strange not to see Auntie Phyllis and Grandad Bob, I think we all missed them, but Mum said that they had a surprise for me, Dad was going for Sister Pascal. She had been moved to a convent in Halifax and was so looking forward to seeing us all again. When she came in and saw me she said, "Ann! How you have grown. I will always remember that first time I saw you. Your father carried you into St. Joseph's church and you must have only been about four years old and such a lovely smile on your face and such a pretty dress. Your Mum has always kept you well dressed and your hair so nice it was a credit to her, and look at you now all grown up."

Auntie Doris had invited some people from the chapel who I knew, they all remarked how well I looked and could see a big improvement in my speech and my movements. It was so good to see all my old friends once more, we visited all our relations and went to see Grandad Dick at their flat. But all too soon it was time for us to say our goodbyes and make our way home, back down south again. Mum promised Doris that she could come and stay with us in the summer holidays, that was something for us both to look forward to.

When I returned to school after the Christmas holidays Sister Quentin asked me if I had been to Lourdes, I told her that I had, but that I was very young. She told me that every Easter they sent six girls with the Bristol Diocese H.C.P.T. that is the 'Handicapped Children's Pilgrims Trust' it was formed in 1956 and every Easter over ten thousand handicapped children are taken to Lourdes. Each person has their own helper they travel by air and overland by train and coach staying in the hotels near the Domain. It is a wonderful experience to be among so many disabled children, and although many are crippled with pain there is a happy atmosphere everywhere.

The daily Mass is a joyful occasion, some of the helpers bring musical instruments with them and we sing happy, rousing hymns. In the hotels at night they have parties and on the last day there is a big fiesta on the prairie which looks across to the grotto. Everyone gets dressed up in fancy costume and has lots of fun. Many of the helpers go every year, they have to pay their own way but look on it as a privilege to help others less fortunate than themselves. I was pleased that I was one of the six girls chosen to go to Lourdes again, it reminded me of being there with Grandad Bob, Mum and Dad.

While I was at home for half term my dad had made an appointment for us to see the Careers Officer at the College. He was called Mr Wood, we had a long talk with him and he suggested that, when I left St. Rose's in July, I should go to Anthony House in Newhaven. He told us that it was a small F.E. unit linked to Chaley Heritage School in East Sussex. They only take sixteen students and work on mobility and independence training and he said it would be ideal for me. Mum and Dad thought it sounded good and asked Mr Wood to arrange an interview for us. We had a letter from the head of the unit, Jean Spears, who suggested that I should come on assessment for two weeks at the end of June, then if it went well, I could start with the other new students in September.

Sister Quentin agreed that it would be good for me to go for two weeks assessment and told me to work hard and to make the most of the opportunity. I was a bit apprehensive about going and did not know what to expect, but I need not have worried. Jean Spears was an exceptionally kind person and in no time at all she had made me feel welcome. It was a friendly place and people were so helpful towards me. Anthony House is about two miles from the town centre of Newhaven up on the hill and overlooks the harbour where the ferry goes across to Dieppe. The views are beautiful, on one side the rolling hills of the Sussex Downs and on the other side across the channel to France.

The house has two large dormitories, one for girls and one for boys, they both sleep eight people. There is a very large lounge overlooking the sea. A dining room and kitchen where the students were taught how to prepare and make snack meals, they called it 'survival cooking'. There was a washing machine to learn how to do their own washing and a workroom.

Jannie and Keith were like house parents and made me welcome and introduced me to the other students, in no time at all I had made friends. It was a hard but enjoyable two weeks. A lovely man called Bill was in charge of the mobility programme and explained what the aim was for each student. At the end of the fortnight Jean told me that I had done well and asked me how I felt about Anthony House, I said that I would love to come and be a student there. Then Jean said I could start in September for two years.

I went back to St. Rose's and told Sister Quentin that I had been accepted at Anthony House and I could go in September for two years, she was very pleased for me and also said that she had sent Jean Spears a very good report on my school work from St. Rose's!

This would be our last few weeks of school, some of the girls were a bit sad at the thoughts of leaving, but we were all determined to enjoy our last school trip and the final disco. Mrs Dove had arranged for all the school leavers to go on a pleasure boat on the canal. It was a lovely sunny day and we did not have to wear our school uniforms so we all put on lovely summer dresses. There was music on the boat and we had a really good time. We stopped at a restaurant on the waterside for lunch which we all enjoyed, while they turned the boat around, then we set off back to school.

On the Friday night we had the leavers' party and disco in the school hall, everyone had a good time, one of the staff had hired a D.J. to run the disco for us and the music was terrific. Mum and Dad came for prize giving and final assembly. It was very emotional, saying goodbye to all my friends, the staff and the Sisters. I had been so happy at St. Rose's and had grown up, now it was time to move on to the next part of my life and to see what that would bring. Dad packed all my things in the car and we set off back to the flat at the college, I was very quiet on the journey thinking back over the last five years and wondering about my future.

Back at the college all the students had gone home for the summer holidays so it was quiet everywhere. Mum told me Auntie Doris was coming down the following Friday for a long holiday with us so that was something to look forward to.

I went with Dad to Guildford to meet Auntie Doris off the coach, it was so good to see her again and for us to be together for a while, we got on so well together and had lots of fun. Mum had a lovely meal waiting when we arrived back at the flat, then I helped Auntie Doris unpack and asked her if she would like to look around the college and plan our holiday.

We had a wonderful time, Dad took us to Southampton to see the Q.E.2. and the Canberra, I did not realise the liners were so big. We went to Portsmouth and saw The Royal Yacht 'Britannia'. Just by Portsmouth in Southsea as you sit on the seafront, you can watch the cross channel ferries coming in and the hovercraft to the Isle of Wight. We went on the hovercraft and spent a day on the Isle of Wight, we also went to Arundel and Chichester and into the New Forest and saw the ponies, then to Bournemouth. We would spend one day at home and the next on a trip out. Time passed quickly, Mum told me we would have to think about what I needed for Newhaven, so we made a list and Auntie Doris came with us into Winchester to do my shopping.

Then we were taking Auntie Doris to Guildford to get the coach back home to Yorkshire. She said that it had been a lovely holiday and good to spend time with us all.

The following Sunday we were packing my things up and setting off for Newhaven and the start of another chapter in my life.

Chapter Nine

The first week of term we spent getting to know everyone, apart from there being fourteen new students, seven boys and seven girls, two new members of staff had arrived. Mary was a teacher and would be running the education part and Teresa was in charge of home care, teaching us how to cook and do our washing and cleaning. The students soon got to know each other and we all seemed to get on so well together. It was a very friendly little group.

At the front of the house there was a large patio and after the evening meal we would sit and talk, it was lovely, you could look over the water and see yachts, sail boats and the ferries coming into the harbour. Jannie and Keith would ask us to talk about ourselves and our backgrounds, this seemed to make it easier for us to understand each other and we were like one large family.

During the day we would work in small groups. Mary would take some of us into the lounge to do maths, mainly it was money management to help us when we went out shopping. She would also show us how to fill in all the forms that you are sent like Income Tax and Disability Allowance and explain about all the household bills, for example:- gas, electric, telephone and rent, so that we would be able to budget our money. It all seemed so complicated but she was very good and tried to make it easy for us.

Teresa would have a group in the workroom teaching them about hygiene in the kitchen, how to prepare snack meals like beans on toast or scrambled eggs. We were taught how to separate the washing, putting whites and coloured clothes in separately and also how to iron.

Bill would take us out on mobility into Newhaven, first to the health centre to get our prescription and then to the chemist. He would also take us to the post office for our allowance and then to do our own shopping. When he thought that we were capable to go on our own, he would get us to phone for our own taxi to go into Newhaven. We did not know it at the time, but he would always follow us and watch how we managed. The shop assistants were very friendly and helpful, I would give them my purse and they would take the money and put the change back in for me.

It was a nice little shopping precinct. The post office was at the top of the hill and I would go in there first to get my allowance, then make my way down to Boots and buy what I needed.

The shop assistant would ask me if I was going to 'Acres the Bakers' which was a bread shop with a snack bar at one end. I would say yes and she would say, "right love I will give them a ring to let them know that you are on your way". I would walk slowly down looking in all the shop windows, it is hard for me to walk down hill. In summer I always had a milk shake, but in winter I would have a hot chocolate and a toasted tea cake. The ladies always made me welcome.

One afternoon when I was chatting to Jean and Mary, Jean asked me if I went to church, I said that I was a Catholic. She told me that she knew a nice couple who might take me to church with them, and she asked them to come and see me. One evening that week they came, they were called Bridie and Derek, what lovely people they were, and we soon became great friends. They told me that they both worked at the hospital in Brighton and lived quite near Anthony House, and would love to take me to church with them. One week we would go to Sunday morning Mass and the next week to the Saturday evening Mass as they worked shifts.

I soon got to know people and made friends at church. A lovely lady called Mrs Sayer told me that she lived near Anthony House and invited me for afternoon tea once a week which I really looked forward to. Then I met a man called John, he was very badly disabled and lived at the Searchlight Centre just up the road from us. He told me that he went to church by taxi and asked me if I would like to go with him? I said, "yes, I would love to." So I started going with John. It also made me think, if John had the courage to go out on his own, so would I.

The next week I asked Bill if I could go into Newhaven by taxi on my own. "Yes Ann you can, but you must book your taxi for both journeys and arrange everything yourself." So that is what I started doing. I seemed to get the same taxi driver every time and he soon got used to me and would help me in and out of his car.

As I got more independent Jean told me that when it was my week to see the doctor, instead of rushing back in time for lunch, I should have it in town and then do my shopping in the afternoon, it would be easier for me and I could take my time. This made me feel so grown up, to be out on my own doing what I wanted.

The only thing was, I dare not tell my parents what I was doing, I knew my mum would be worried sick if she knew that I was walking around outside on my own. I did have one or two falls but luckily no harm was done, and it only made me work harder for my independence.

There was a work centre in Newhaven and Jean encouraged us all to attend for work experience, we took it in turns to go there. I tried it for a while but found it very difficult to do the jobs they required because of my hands, so Jean told me to stay at home and work on my independence. I went out more with Bill into Newhaven, I used to get very upset because I could not use my hands but Bill would say to me; "never mind Ann, things will get better for you in time." Some days I would get rather low about my hand movements and wonder if I would improve.

At the weekends Jannie and Keith would take us out in the bus. Brighton was only nine miles away and Eastbourne fourteen miles the other way. I liked shopping in Eastbourne best, there are some lovely shops, on my way back we would sit on top of Beachy Head, it is a magnificent view from there.

Sometimes Keith would take the boys to the football match in Brighton, and he would drop the girls off with Jannie to do our own thing. Then we would all meet up together for a meal before going home.

Mary would organise outings into London to shows and the museums, I liked the National History Museum best. We went to see shows like 'Annie' and 'Barnum' and the Royal Tournament at Earls Court which I really enjoyed. At Christmas time they took us shopping into London and to see the lights and the big Christmas tree in Trafalgar Square. Keith took us to Brands Hatch Motor Racing, that was a bit noisy for me!!

We had our Christmas party and disco, Jean invited some students from Chaley Heritage School and told us we could invite any friends, so I asked Bridie and Derek to come. We all enjoyed ourselves. Bill made some punch, not too potent, but it did make us feel happy. Then it was time to go home for the Christmas holidays.

I spent a quiet Christmas at the flat at the college and then we went to Yorkshire for New Year. It was good to see Auntie Doris again, and we had a lot of time together telling her all about Newhaven. What I was doing, going out on my own shopping, and about all the friends that I had made. She was so pleased for me and told me that she had never seen me look so well and happy.

All too soon it was time to go back to Hampshire and for me to get ready for another term at Newhaven.

One Sunday in spring Keith had taken us on a mystery run into the countryside and we stopped for lunch at a beautiful little village called Alfriston. It had a Wild Fowl Reserve and the streams zig-zagged their way down the river and on into the sea, you can see all kinds of birds there. We sat for quite a while as it was so peaceful. On our way back Keith told us that he wanted to call at the old fort at the top of Newhaven, he had heard that it had been refurbished and he wanted to see what they had done. As we got near you could see that they had made a car park at one side, so we pulled in and got out to have a look round. Keith said that the fort was very old and during the last war it had been used as a lookout post, but since then it had been neglected and left in disrepair. Now it was going to be re-opened again. They had put all new seats around with a little café at one end and a bandstand at the other end. We saw a notice in the café window advertising Band Concerts, Sunday afternoons 2.00 p.m. to 4.00 p.m., weather permitting. Keith said that if anyone wanted to go he would take us the following Sunday afternoon.

That was the start of another phase in my life at Newhaven, I have always liked music of any kind and enjoyed listening to it. Keith took us up to the fort the following Sunday. While we sat listening to the band I asked Keith, if no-one else wanted to come up here, would it be alright if I ordered a taxi and came on my own? Keith said he would ask Jean and see what she thought, if she said yes I could go on my own. So that is what I used to do. After

Sunday lunch I would phone my favourite taxi man and ask him to pick me up at 1.45 p.m. and take me up to the fort and collect me again at 4.15 p.m. The best thing was there were no steps so I felt quite confident. The staff in the café soon got used to me and as time went by I began to meet people and it was nice to sit and chat. Those were very happy times.

That summer, just before end of term, Jean told us that she had booked a day trip across to Dieppe on the ferry for everyone, both staff and students. That would mean each of us would have someone to push our wheelchairs. We had to be up early as the ferry left Newhaven at 6.30 a.m. so we just had tea and toast for breakfast, Jean said we would have a meal on the boat.

It was a good crossing and as we approached the French coast we all went up on deck. What a wonderful sight it was, we could see the harbour and across the countryside to the town of Dieppe. After we had disembarked we had a stroll around the harbour and then had a coffee at one of the many little cafes, we sat outside and two nice young French men came to take our orders. Keith said, "now girls, no getting off with the waiters!" We all had a good laugh.

Jean told us that she had booked a meal for us all in a restaurant, then we were going to the hypermarket for our duty free shopping before joining the ferry home. "So enjoy yourselves and we meet back at 4.30 p.m. that should give us plenty of time to catch the ferry."

Jannie asked me if I would like her to take me, I said, "Oh yes please," so we set off to explore the town. Dieppe is not a very large town, the main part seemed to be the harbour and the docks, with cargo boats and small fishing vessels coming and going. It is very picturesque with narrow winding streets with pavement cafés and bars. We had to walk with my wheelchair in the road most of the time.

We looked around one or two shops for souvenirs but Jannie said they were too expensive and said we should wait until we got to the hypermarket. We walked a little way up the hill out of town and looked around a very old church with some beautiful statues of Our

Lady and the saints. Then we just sat for a while looking out over the harbour and talking until it was time to go and meet everyone else and have our meal.

It was a very good restaurant and we all enjoyed a lovely meal with wine flowing freely. No one fancied the frogs legs, I had chicken in a wine sauce, 'superb'. The sweets trolley was full of fresh cream cakes and gateaux, they tasted delicious. Jean said, "I hope you are all capable of going round the hypermarket?"

"The walk will do us good before we get on the ferry for home." Bill replied.

I had heard people talk about the hypermarkets, but until you go inside one, you do not realize just how large they are, I think I could have spent all day in there looking round. We all bought our duty free goods, I bought Mum a lovely scarf and some expensive perfume, I bought myself some too, and a bottle of brandy for my Dad. I think everyone bought cigarettes, even though not many of us smoked, but to take home for friends as they were so much cheaper than in England.

Then it was time to head for the harbour and board the ferry, that was when the trouble began, the man at the gate would not let us through in our wheelchairs. He told Jean that we should not have been allowed on in Newhaven, it was against company regulations. Bill came forward, he spoke very good French and told him we all had passports and tickets and there was no reason why we should not get on board. He was letting everyone else through except our party. We must have been there over half an hour and everyone was on board when the harbour police and the captain of the ferry arrived. Finally, after a very heated discussion, we were allowed onto the ferry. We were all very relieved as we settled down for the crossing home, some of the other passengers were upset at the way we had been treated and told us not to take any notice of the silly French official and hoped we had had an enjoyable day out. As we sailed into Newhaven we were all a little weary and ready for home. Jean said we could have an extra hour in bed next morning. We all thanked her very much for taking us out for the day.

I had a good summer holiday at home, we went up to Yorkshire for a week to see Auntie Doris and our friends. When we came back we went house hunting as Mum was a bit fed up living in the flat and wanted to be amongst people and where she could walk to the shops. So we travelled around the villages and towns around Alton looking at different houses. Dad said he was surprised how expensive property was down south compared with the north. We had sold our large bungalow for twelve thousand pounds, but there was nothing around for less than twenty five thousand. It was a big worry for them. They still had not found anywhere when I went to Newhaven in September. Mum told me not to worry, something would turn up, but I knew she was worried.

I soon got back into a routine again going out with Bill and on my own in Newhaven. John at the Searchlight Centre would invite me up on a Thursday afternoon for a chat and a cup of tea, and I began to mix with some of the other residents there.

At home the boys would tease me about the football, my Dad was a Leeds United fan, they had a good team in the seventies and I would say, "Brighton are rubbish". One Saturday they kept on at me so much I said, "right, I am coming with you and I will cheer for the other team." I have never been to a professional football match and I really enjoyed the cheering and shouting that went on between the supporters. When the boys saw how much I enjoyed the match one of them said, "Ann you will have to come with us every time," and I did. I even bought a blue and white Brighton scarf which I wore at every game.

One Monday after I had been into Newhaven on my own and had my lunch out, I arrived back home where Jean came out to meet me and said, "Ann, you have a visitor waiting for you." When I went inside Mr Love, my social worker from Winchester, was sitting in the lounge with a cup of coffee in his hand. "Hello stranger, so this is what you get up to when you are away from home?" he said.

I have been very fortunate and had very good social workers and Mr Love was one of the best. I sat with him and we had a long talk about how I was managing at Anthony House. I told him all about what I was doing, about my independence and that I was very happy there. He was pleased for me and said he would call and see Mum and Dad and say how happy I was there. I said, "Please don't tell Mum about me going out on my own into Newhaven, she will only worry about me."

"All right Ann I won't," he said, "it is just nice to see you happy and working so hard here."

I began to think about my birthday coming up in the next month and wondered what I should do about it, I would be eighteen this year everyone seemed to make it a special one now, not at twenty one like they used to.

I was sat with Jannie one evening talking about it when Derek and Bridie called to see me. Derek asked, "What day is it Ann?"

I told him it would be on a Saturday in three weeks time. He looked in his diary and said, "you are lucky Ann, that is our weekend off." If your Mum and Dad can get through they can stay at our house for the weekend. So that is what we arranged. Mum was so pleased we could all be together for this special time. Dad said they would get away early on the Friday and should arrive about seven at night. He talked to Derek on the phone and asked him if he would be kind enough to book a meal at a good restaurant for us all on the Saturday night.

It was lovely to see Mum and Dad again, my Dad gave me a bunch of red roses and a hug. Mum said, "we have another surprise Ann, we have found a bungalow and move in next week."

Before I had chance to ask about it Bridie and Derek arrived. I introduced Mum and Dad and they all got on well. Mum told us about the new bungalow, she'd seen it advertised in the local paper and they went straight round to look at it. An old couple had it but they were having to go into a home as they could not manage now and wanted a quick sale. Dad made them an offer which they accepted. Mum said that it needed a lot of work and money spending on it but they could make it into a home for us all.

Then Derek told Dad to follow him back to their house, Mum told me to be ready for ten next morning as we were going shopping into Eastbourne. Next day, we had a good day out looking around the shops

"If we are going to a posh restaurant tonight," Mum said, "let's see if we can find a nice dress for you to wear."

After going in quite a few shops I chose a red dress with long sleeves which I could also wear at our Christmas party. Then my Dad took me into a large jewellers and bought me a beautiful gold watch for my birthday. I was overwhelmed and did not know what to say.

Mum came back with me and helped me to get ready for the evening out, she said that I looked quite grown up in my new dress and some make up, I felt a little older too. Bridie and Derek arrived and we set off for the restaurant. We had a super birthday meal and a bottle of wine to celebrate my coming of age. I was glad we all got on so well together and had an enjoyable evening out.

Dad picked me up for church the next morning and after Mass I introduced them to John, Mrs Sayer and one or two more people I had got to know, then we went back to Anthony House for lunch. Mum said they were going straight back after lunch as she was on duty that night but, she added, Dad would collect me and bring me to our new bungalow for the Christmas holidays. After they had gone Jannie and Keith came and told me, as a birthday treat, they were going to take me up to London that afternoon to see the Christmas lights, then we'd have a meal out on our way back as their birthday present to me. It had certainly been a special weekend for me, and an eighteenth birthday to remember.

I was very excited going home with Dad for the Christmas break. He was telling me about Alresford, it is a small old town, the houses and shops all have a character of their own. A river runs at the bottom of the Dean with trout fishing and there is a steam railway just like we had in Keighley.

As you approach Alresford you drive down a tree lined avenue with wide grass verges at each side. The main street ahead was decorated with fairy lights and every shop and house had a Christmas tree hung from the upstairs window. What a wonderful sight it was, I said to Dad that I thought Mum would be happy there and settle down now.

Our bungalow was in a small close just off the Dean, where the river ran by and only five minutes walk from the shops. Mum said, "we will have a lot of work to do as it has been very neglected but we can make it into a home for us."

We had a quiet Christmas together, we found the church and went to Mass and had a walk around the town. There were three hotels that served meals, we liked the look of the Swan and had a meal there. One day we went out and bought wallpaper and paint for both bedrooms. "Next time you are home your room will be decorated for you," Dad said. There was a heavy snowfall just before I went back to Newhaven, but in two days it had all cleared away. I was looking forward to going back and seeing all my friends again.

The boys were very excited when I arrived, they told me that Brighton had won all their cup games so far, and they asked me if I was going with them on Saturday, it was another cup game. I said that I would love to join them. "If we keep on like this we might even get to Wembley," Keith said.

A few weeks later Jean had a meeting with everyone, she'd had a letter from the Bursar at Chaley Heritage asking us to help them in a fund raising effort. After a lot of discussion it was decided we would all do a sponsored walk. Keith and Bill both thought that Seaford seafront would be ideal as it was just half a mile long and it was flat. Everyone could do their own thing. The boys were aiming for five miles in their wheelchairs, some even said they would try ten miles. Jannie asked me what I was going to do, I said that I wanted to try and walk one mile!!

It was arranged for the sponsored walk to be on a Sunday morning at the beginning of March. I went to the Saturday evening Mass because I knew that I would be too tired after the walk.

It was a nice sunny day with just a slight breeze, the staff had brought flasks of coffee and soup and marked off half a mile on the seafront. They let the wheelchairs start first at five minute intervals and then the walkers, some of the staff walked with us in case anyone fell or wanted a rest. Some had collecting tins and went amongst the people who had come to watch. They were shouting encouragement all the time. Although it was hard work we all enjoyed ourselves. If someone wanted to stop the crowd would shout, "come on, you are nearly there you can do it." We raised quite a lot of money that day and every one of us felt a great sense of achievement in reaching our own target.

When we had all finished Keith went into Newhaven for a takeaway for us. I can remember back at home we were all sitting in the lounge with our feet in bowls of water and Jannie came round with a jar of ointment, rubbing it on our feet and legs. It did look comical, we just relaxed for the rest of that day.

Chapter Ten

One evening Derek called to see me, he had been to a meeting at church about going to see the Pope when he came to England in May. He asked me if I would like to join them, they were booking a coach to go to Gatwick Airport if John and I wanted we could go with them, I said that I would love to go. So Derek said that he would put my name on the list.

I did not know then but May 1982 was going to be a memorable time for me. Brighton football team won through to the Cup Final and Keith managed to get tickets for us, so we were off to Wembley to see the Cup Final: Brighton versus Liverpool.

What a wonderful experience that was, the atmosphere was unbelievable. I had never seen so many people, there were crowds everywhere. When you are inside, the noise from the singing and the massed bands playing as the two teams come out onto the pitch, the roar that goes up is so exciting. Most people said that Brighton had no chance of winning, but we played very well and it ended in a two all draw. Unfortunately we lost the replay in midweek, we could only watch that on television at home. When I told my Dad that I had been to the Cup Final at Wembley he was very jealous, but also so happy for me that I had had the opportunity to go.

Two weeks later, Friday 29th May 1982 marked an historic event in English history. Pope John Paul II was coming to the United Kingdom, the first time ever for the head of the Roman Catholic Church to visit our country.

I will always remember the day he arrived, Derek told me he would pick me up at 5.30 a.m. Then collect John and take us to the car park where the coach was, they had to be at Gatwick Airport for 6.30 a.m. I had asked Jean about going and she had told me I could. "But you are on your own, you will need to be up at 4.30 a.m. to get yourself ready in time and have your breakfast." It was quite an ordeal for me and, even though I laddered two pair of tights getting dressed, I made it!

The coach arrived on time and we were soon on our way to Gatwick and were met by police and shown where to park. The Pope was not arriving until 8.0 a.m. but everyone had to be in place well before then, our group had been lucky and had tickets on the front row out on the tarmac, near where the aircraft would land.

What a wonderful sight as the plane came to rest and the doors opened and Pope John Paul stood at the top of the steps in all his vestments and blessed everyone. He then came down the steps and stood on the tarmac and said in English. "This is a very memorable moment for everyone." Then he knelt down and kissed the ground.

After being welcomed by many dignitaries he came across to meet the people, as he passed by he touched a head or face. When he came to me he smiled and touched my face and said a few words, I was so overcome with emotion. I can't remember what he said. I would like to think it was that he had remembered me! But maybe that is wishful thinking.

Going back in the coach we talked about the wonderful time and experience that we had all shared together, it was another golden moment for me to lock away and to remember all my life.

That evening as we watched the news on television it showed pictures of the Pope's arrival, and as the cameras followed his movements, I could see myself and our group there. I followed the Holy Father as he toured the United Kingdom in his 'Pope mobile' saying Mass to the many thousands of people who had gathered where he went.

As we came near to the end of term I suddenly realised that this was the final phase of my school education. I looked back to my early years at Lister Lane School, at St. Rose's boarding school in Stroud, and now at Anthony House, Newhaven. I have been very fortunate and had some very good teachers and helpers and it is because of them that I have improved more than I ever thought I would.

I was a little sad the day Dad came to take me home, saying goodbye to all my friends at church and at the centre. Jean told me that I had worked hard, then everyone came out to wave me off. I was going home to live with Mum and Dad.

I soon settled in at home living with Mum and Dad again, getting to know the neighbours around the close where we lived.

One day Mr Love, my social worker called to see me to talk about what I was going to do now I was at home. He suggested taking me down to the Hexagon Centre near Southampton to have a look around and see if it was suitable for me to attend there. He said it was a work centre for physically handicapped people from the age of 18 years upwards.

When we arrived and I saw the shape of the building I understood why it was called the Hexagon Centre. As soon as we went inside you could feel the happy atmosphere everywhere. Mr Love took me to meet the manageress, Mrs Hancock. She was a tall lady with dark hair and a pleasant smile, she soon put me at ease. She asked me what I had been doing at Anthony House, and then told me about the centre and the many things they did there.

After we all had a chat and a coffee she took us to look around the centre and introduced me to some of the staff and clients. One half of the centre was for the heavy type of work like woodwork, metal work and printing. At the other end there was photography, art, craft and clerical work, outside there were two greenhouses and quite a large garden centre. There was also a hairdressers, a coffee bar and a canteen where lunch was served daily. A group of ladies had a small shop which opened a few hours every day and visitors could buy things made at the centre.

We then went back to Mrs Hancock's office and she asked me what I would like to do if I went there. I said, "I would go for clerical work and try my hand at needlework in the craft section. Mrs Hancock suggested that I went on a month's trial to see how I coped with the work and travelling every day. My Dad asked how I would get there from Alresford? Mrs Hancock said that they ran a bus to pick clients up in the Winchester area and also from the hospital. Mr Love said that he would arrange for a taxi to collect me from Alresford and take me to Winchester Hospital in the morning and pick me up at night and take me home again. It was arranged that I would go four days a week to start on Monday 22nd August and have Thursdays at home. Mr Love reassured me that it was a very good centre and all the staff would help me settle and get used to the work

"A taxi will call for you at 7.50 a.m. and you should be home for 5.00 p.m. each evening," he said. "I will call and see you in two weeks to hear how you are getting on."

On my first day Mum woke me with a cup of tea at 6.50 a.m. and asked me how I was? I said I had a funny feeling in my tummy. She said that she would help me get ready as the taxi was coming at 7.50 a.m. Both Mum and Dad gave me a big hug and said that they would be thinking of me all day and told me not to worry and just do my best. Then we heard a car horn blow, a kind man got out of a car and asked for Ann Whitaker? He said, "I am Mr Reumen, your taxi driver and will take you to Winchester Hospital". He helped me into his car, Mum and Dad waved me off and he drove away. He asked me if I liked music, I said that I did and he put a tape on, and said, "I like all kinds of music and have about fifty tapes in the car, so I am sure you will like some of them." Mr. Reumen seemed to know all the back roads and it did not take long before he was pulling into the reception area of Winchester Hospital. He helped me out of the car and took me inside and told the lady at the desk my name and that I was waiting for the bus to the Hexagon Centre. He asked the ladies to keep an eye on me and said, "I will be here to pick you up at 4.45 p.m."

It was not long before a blue bus pulled into the area and a handsome, young man came in and asked if I was Ann Whitaker? When I said I was, he said, "I'm Robin your driver". He then helped me onto the bus and introduced me to the other people, they were a friendly group and soon made me feel at ease. Robin told us we had only two more clients to collect then it would be off to the Hexagon. He had a country and western music tape on, one of the clients said to me, "You will have to get used to the noise, that's all Robin likes." And everyone laughed.

We seemed to travel out into the country to pick up two more people and then across the bypass through Chandlers Ford to Eastleigh where the Hexagon Centre is. I was surprised to see four more buses and people being helped into the centre. You have to book in at the office as soon as you get inside and, as I was new,

Robin took me to Mrs Hancock's office and she asked me to sit down, then a tall man came in and introduced himself. "I am Mr Wilson the Deputy Manager, I hope you will like it here, we are a friendly group and I am sure you will be happy working with us".

Mrs Hancock took me to meet Mrs Doulas, the needlework instructor, and Mrs Wilton, the clerical instructor, and told me I would spend the day with them. They were both extremely nice ladies. Mrs Doulas was short with white hair and always smiling while Mrs Wilton was tall with dark brown hair, wore spectacles and dressed very smart, she had a quiet, gentle voice. As they introduced me to the other clients, Mrs Doulas asked Maxine, a coloured girl about my age, to look after me and show me where everything was and where to put my things. Maxine and I soon became friends and got on so well together, in no time at all I settled down and felt at ease there.

We stopped for a coffee break at 10.30 a.m. for 20 minutes. Maxine asked me what I was doing for lunch, she said the canteen did a main meal or just a snack and sandwiches. I told her I would just have a sandwich as Mum would have a hot meal waiting for me in the evening. She told me, when you book-in in the morning, you have to buy your ticket for lunch, then the kitchen know how many meals to make each day. Lunch break was from 12.30 p.m. until 1.30 p.m. It was an enjoyable hour, relaxing and chatting to each other.

In the afternoon I was with Mrs Wilton in clerical, everyone called her Shirley, she asked if I had done typing before, when I said I had, she got me some work to do and watched how I got on. It seemed no time at all before Shirley told us to tidy our work and get ready for home as the buses left at 4.00 p.m.

On my way to the entrance Mrs Hancock came across and asked me how my first day had been. I told her I had enjoyed it and would be very happy to attend daily. She was pleased and said she looked forward to seeing me in the morning and giving me my new timetable for the week.

Robin helped us all into his bus and set off, dropping clients along the way to Winchester arriving at the hospital where Mr Reumins was waiting for me. He helped me into his car and said we would be taking a different route home to avoid the teatime traffic. Then he asked me about my first day at the Hexagon, I said that I had quite enjoyed myself meeting new people and that I was sure I would soon make friends.

Mum was waiting at the door for me as Mr Reumins helped me out of the car and said he would see me in the morning as he drove away. Mum took me into the kitchen and I had a cup of tea and told her about my day while she got the evening meal ready. When Dad came home we sat around the table and had our meal, and I told them about meeting people at Winchester Hospital and how friendly everyone was, and the bus journey with Robin. There was a boy about my age called Nick who we picked up just outside Winchester. He had cerebral palsy like me but was more disabled and in a wheelchair all the time. I told them about Maxine, the girl who had helped me and shown me where everything was, I knew we would be good friends in time.

Mum could see I was getting tired and while Dad cleared away and washed up, Mum bathed me and got me ready for bed, and then told me to relax and watch TV for a while as I had an early start the next day. That seemed to be my routine on the days that I went to the centre, I needed the extra rest as the travel and work seemed to make me more tired.

Thursday was my day off so Mum let me sleep in and I did not get up until about 8.30 a.m., and then I had a quiet morning at home. In the afternoon we went shopping together in Alresford, I found the people in the shops were so very friendly and helpful. Mum would take me into a small café called "The Tiffin Bar". Rosemary and Angela the two waitresses were really nice to me and treated me just like everyone else, it made me feel normal! Sometimes when I am out, people tend to talk over my head and treat me as if I cannot understand, they say things like; "would she like a sweet?", instead of asking me. That makes Mum and I so angry and Mum will reply, "why not ask Ann if she wants a sweet, she can talk for herself.", but these people mean well, it is difficult for them to understand. Alresford is a very pretty town with a lot of character all of its own. Each shop is different and many are very old and have not been modernised and spoilt like in some towns.

There was a small market on Thursday in Broad Street and also the Women's Institute had stalls in the Community Centre, selling homemade cakes and jams, fresh eggs and flowers and bric-a-brac. I loved going in there talking to the ladies while Mum bought cakes and jam. I soon got to know people, even Doctor Tanner, my doctor, if he saw me he would call out or wave to me in the street, I felt at home and happy being out with Mum on our own.

I had only been at the Hexagon Centre four weeks when one afternoon I slipped and fell on my right arm, Mrs Hancock and Mr Wilson took me to Winchester Hospital. After I had had an x-ray, it showed that it was broken in three places and they put it in plaster from my wrist to my shoulder. Mrs Hancock phoned my Mum and told her not to worry as they were looking after me and would bring me home from the hospital as soon as I was ready to leave. My arm felt so heavy with the plaster cast on, they put a sling on for me to hold it up. Then Mrs Hancock and Mr Wilson took me home. Mum was nearly in tears when she saw how much pain I was in. Mrs Hancock was very apologetic about my fall and told Mum how brave I had been, I did not cry at all. Mr Wilson said, "Ann was just glad that it was her right arm that was broken and not her left as she is left handed."

I stayed at home for two weeks and had to use my wheelchair, as I felt unsteady with the pot on my arm. It was hard work for mum as she had to bath and dress me all the time. Mum put a bin liner over my plaster cast while I was in the bath to try and keep it dry. After a couple of weeks at home I felt better and Dad phoned the Hexagon Centre to see if I could go with my arm in plaster? They said that I could, and one of the care assistants would be there to help me whenever I needed it.

I started back at the centre using my wheelchair all the time, it was about eight weeks before I had to go back to the hospital and have the plaster cast removed. My arm had healed and the bones all set again but it felt stiff. The doctor told Mum that some physiotherapy would help to get my joints moving again. While we were waiting in the reception area for our taxi home, Mum saw a poster advertising, "The Pinder's Centre" Physiotherapy and

Hydrotherapy treatment with fully trained staff, she wrote down the phone number and address, it was in a small village called Ovington.

When we got home Mum phoned and asked if we could go and have a look around to see if they could take me. A nice lady called Teresa told Mum all about the centre and said that one of the physiotherapists, called Elizabeth, could fit me in on a Thursday morning at 10.30 a.m. Mum told her that it would be fine and we would attend the following Thursday.

The next day, Mum was having her hair done and was asking Joan, her hairdresser, about 'The Pinder's Centre'. Joan told Mum one of her ladies used to go for treatment there and said it was an excellent place. Joan also told her to contact Mrs Shaw, she was the co-ordinator for all the voluntary work in Alresford and would organise someone to take me to the Centre. Mum had a chat with Mrs Shaw and it was arranged that a man called Mr Buxton would call for us and take us there the following Thursday.

That was the start of another weekly routine and making new friends. I became very fond of Mr Buxton, he was a retired church minister who lived just a few minutes walk from our house and he was a very kind man indeed. He had a dog called Tristan and while Mum took me in for my treatment Mr Buxton would take Tristan for a walk.

Teresa met us in reception and took us through and introduced us to Elizabeth who would be treating me. She asked Mum about my injury and Mum told her about my broken arm and said the doctor had suggested some therapy to strengthen the joints. While Elizabeth was working on my shoulder and arm she was telling us about the types of treatment they did at the centre. She also asked me about my disability and I told her that I had had both physiotherapy and hydrotherapy since starting school. When Elizabeth had finished my treatment she asked Mum to take me through to the hydro pool. I was surprised to see how large the pool was.

Elizabeth explained about the hydro pool and the wave motion action and suggested that I try it next time. So the following week I went prepared with my bathing costume and did all my exercises in the pool. The water was lovely and warm it seemed to take no effort moving my arms and legs about, then when Elizabeth had finished she put a rubber ring round me and let me have a swim for ten minutes on my own. I felt so relaxed when I came out it was a wonderful feeling. So that is what we did every week and I really enjoyed it and it helped my movements too.

Mr Buxton became a dear friend of ours, sometimes he would take us back to his house for coffee, in the nice weather he would take us for a run around the countryside. I loved the spring time seeing the wild flowers and trees coming into bloom and the little lambs jumping about in the fields.

Elizabeth told us that she was a bell ringer at St. John's Church in Alresford and explained all about the bells and the different chimes they could do. We could hear the bells in our bungalow and Mum would say on a Friday night, "Can you hear Elizabeth ringing the bells?" It was practice night.

At the beginning of November Mum was not well and the doctor told her that she would have to go into Winchester Hospital for an operation. Mr Love, my social worker, suggested that I stay with a family in Chandlers Ford while Mum was in hospital then she would not worry about me as much. So that is what I did, that way I could still attend the Hexagon Centre every day. My Dad came to visit me after he had seen Mum in hospital and told me not to worry, she was getting on fine after her operation.

The family I stayed with Mr and Mrs Powell were very kind people. They took me to church in Eastleigh on the Sunday and after Mass one of the nuns came over to talk to me. Sister Ann Joseph from the Convent in Fair Oak told me there was just four Sisters now. She had been a head teacher in Eastleigh but was now retired. Mrs Powell explained that I was just staying with them while Mum was in hospital. Sister said she would collect me and take me to the convent for tea and show me round. Both Mum and Dad often say to me, "Ann, you have gathered more friends around you than anyone we know." Dad says, "it must be that wonderful smile you always have that attracts them."

Luckily, Mum was soon well again and able to go home from

hospital, and a few days later Dad came to take me back home. He thanked Mr and Mrs Powell for looking after me and told them it had been a big help, knowing I was there with them.

It was getting close to Christmas and Mum said that she did not feel like travelling all the way up to Yorkshire so soon after being in hospital so we had a quiet time just on our own. At the Hexagon Centre we had a lovely Christmas lunch and in the afternoon the staff put on a pantomime for all the clients, every one enjoyed themselves and had a good time.

Early in the New Year, Mum was taken ill again. After seeing Mr Lane a specialist at Winchester hospital, he sent her to see a chest specialist, Mr Lee in Southampton hospital. After examining Mum, they took a biopsy which revealed a growth in her lung. Mr Lee wanted to admit her as soon as possible for an operation.

Mr Love told us that Mrs Powell was unable to take me while Mum was in hospital, but he told us a very good friend of his called Jackie, who also lived in Chandlers Ford, would look after me. He said they are a lovely family with a young boy of their own and I could stay with them as long as it was necessary.

Dad took me to stay with Jackie, after settling me in, he told me not to worry about Mum, everything would be fine. The next day she was admitted into Southampton hospital where they were going to do tests to see how advanced the growth was.

My Dad called to see me on his way back from the hospital, I could see that he was very worried about her. He told me they would not know anything for twenty four hours, when the results of the tests would be known. "All we can do is say our prayers for Mum and hope all goes well for her." I tried to keep cheerful for Dad, but as soon as he left I broke down and could not stop crying.

Jackie was very good to me, she phoned our own doctor in Alresford and explained how distressed I was about Mum. He told her to increase my medication at night time so I would sleep, and she could call him anytime if she was worried about me.

I continued going to the Hexagon Centre every day, Mr Love explained to Mrs Hancock about Mum and everyone at the centre was very kind to me, trying to take my mind off it. I think being

81

with my friends helped, but on the day of Mum's operation I could not settle at all. I knew she was first on Mr Lee's list for her operation at 8.30 a.m., but we did not know how long she would be in theatre. Mrs Hancock said that she would phone the hospital after lunch at 1.00 p.m. and see if there was any news. I knew by the smile on her face when she came to see me that it was good news. They had been able to remove one of Mum's lungs and all the cancerous cells. Mum was in a satisfactory condition and all would be well.

My Dad called that night and told me that Mum was awake but had tubes and bottles everywhere. He had spoken to the doctor who had told him that the operation had gone well. They had removed all the cancer, Mum was clear, and she did not require any chemotherapy or radiotherapy, just lots of rest and plenty of T.L.C. Dad said he would call for me the following evening and take me to see her. It was such a relief to know that she was going to be all right, I just burst into tears. Dad gave me a cuddle and told me that I had been very brave and would take me to see her the next evening.

We continued visiting every day for two weeks and could see her health improving. She was walking about after three days determined to go home. She was always in trouble for asking to be discharged, in the end the surgeon gave in, on one condition; she had a home help.

We were overjoyed and within five days she had me back home. Three months passed, with the home help and support from neighbours and friends, Mum was fit and well and after all these years the cancer hasn't returned.

It was lovely to be back home with Mum and Dad. We tried to help her all we could and make sure that she had plenty of rest.

Our Parish Priest, Father Spencer, was very good to Mum, he used to visit her regularly and sit and chat with her. It was Father Spencer who told Mum to contact Nancy Hill at St. Peter's Church in Winchester. He told her that she did a lot of work with the disabled and she was the leader of the "Faith and Light" group in Winchester and that it would be good for me to join and meet more people.

Mum phoned Nancy Hill and she said that she would come through to Alresford to see us and tell us about "Faith and Light".

Nancy was a very nice person she was a retired school teacher and now seemed to spend most of her time working with the church.

She organised the annual Parish Pilgrimage to Lourdes on the 'Across' bus which was for the elderly, sick, and disabled people. The 'Across' is a National Charity which began forty years ago. They have special buses that can take stretcher cases and wheelchairs. The group is made up of a doctor, nurses, helpers and a priest, to look after the sick pilgrims, both on the journey, and during their stay in Lourdes.

Nancy told me about Faith and Light. It is for mentally and physically disabled people who meet together with able bodied helpers once a month in a Christian surrounding to try and understand more about Christ's teachings. In the summer they have a holiday together with other groups from different parts of the country. Nancy told me that this year Winchester group would be organising the holiday and about sixty people would be coming to Park Place Pastoral Centre in Wickham, near Winchester for a week at the end of July. She said they were fortunate in their group as there were six girls about my age who attended regularly and was sure that I would enjoy the meetings.

I thanked Nancy for coming to see me and told her that Dad would take me to their meeting on Sunday afternoon. The people were friendly and I soon felt at ease, especially with Margaret, Helen, Susan and Louise. They had all left school and were waiting to go on to college or university. We had great fun together, they loved pushing me in my wheel chair, running fast with me and laughing all the time. We seemed to get on so well it did not matter that I was disabled, they treated me as an equal they told me about the holidays or 'Fiesta' as they are called, and said it is great to meet up with old friends again and the fun they all have.

Helen told me about the annual weekend in Walsingham every September where there can be up to five hundred Faith and Light members together for the weekend. Walsingham is a shrine to 'Our Lady' and it holds a special place in our lives. Also every December they gather together in London to sing carols around the big Christmas tree in Trafalgar Square. Groups travel from all over the country to take part in these special events.

I looked forward to the Faith and Light, we held them in the church hall at St. Peter's, on other occasions we met at one of the leader's homes or arranged to meet with another group from around the diocese.

With going to the Hexagon Centre four days a week, the Pinder's Centre on a Thursday and making new friends at Faith and Light, I felt that my life was working out well. I loved living in Alresford with Mum and Dad, people were getting used to me and would stop and talk and were very friendly. On a Sunday after morning Mass we would go to the Swan Hotel for lunch. The chef, Steve, always had a joke with me and asked if I wanted one of his specials. He said he made cottage pie just for me! Then I had a large slice of chocolate gateaux to finish with. After lunch we would walk around Alresford or along the riverside. The water was so clear you could see the large trout swimming around.

There were swans and ducks too, it was lovely in the Springtime when the little ducklings were swimming in a line with their mum, it was so peaceful. I liked to see the old thatched cottages and farmhouses. Across from the river there were fields of watercress beds.

Alresford is well known from growing watercress, it is sent all over the country. Along the other side of the town is the railway. The line was closed down years ago but recently the local people began to renovate the station, the track and the engines. The line is open again at weekends from Alresford to Alton. It is nice to see the old steam engines pulling coaches along the track, it is called the 'Water Cress Line' and it is often seen on TV in old time drama productions and films.

Chapter Eleven

The week that I spent at Park Place with Faith and Light was a new experience for me, it was nice to meet old friends from the North of England and make more friends with both the helpers and the disabled members.

Nancy had organised the week well with outings every day or members could just stay at Park Place. We went to Chichester with its lovely cathedral and Arundel with a boat trip by the castle to view all the wild fowl. Portsmouth and a trip round the Naval Base with many war ships as well as the Royal Yacht Britannia, which looked marvellous, and Southsea with time to spend on the fun fair.

When we returned for our evening meal and a short prayer meeting, some people had brought guitars and we would sit outside in the grounds and have a sing-song, or they would entertain us.

Nancy introduced me to the Sisters who ran Park Place Pastoral Centre, there are six Franciscan nuns who came from India. Originally the building was a girl's boarding school that belonged to the diocese which had closed down in the late 1960's. After a large amount of alterations the Bishop of Portsmouth asked the Sisters to come over from India and run it as a centre where groups of people could come on retreat for reflection and prayer.

The house is set in some beautiful woodland grounds away from the busy road, it is so peaceful and relaxing you feel as though you are in a different world. They have built a new chapel onto the original building and, as you sit there you feel at peace, I spent quite a lot of time there.

Sister Evelyn, who is in charge, told me that they hold prayer weekends during the year and special visitor day vigils at Easter and Christmas. She said I would be welcome anytime, and thought maybe my Mum could come with me to one of the meetings and meet everyone.

The last night of the holiday is called 'Fiesta night' where everybody dresses up in costume to a special theme, each group has to perform a piece within the theme. We then end up with a barbecue and a sing-song and thanksgiving prayers for everyone who has made this week so special for us all.

When I told Mum about Park Place and the wonderful feeling you get just being there, she said that she would love to go with me for the weekend in September and meet the Sisters. That is what we did and, after Mum had had a talk with the Sisters, we joined and became members and friends of Park Place.

Now although I am living in Lancashire Sister Evelyn and I still write to each other, and I go down and spend about ten days with them every summer and I always come back refreshed in mind and spirit.

I was out with Mum on Saturday afternoon, shopping in Alresford, as we walked by the community centre people were going inside. Mum said to me "I wonder what's going on there today, shall we go in and have a look?"

Inside we saw a group of people handing out leaflets and information about evening classes due to start in September at Perins High School, Alresford. A lovely lady came across to talk to us and explained that, as well as the evening classes, they could also arrange one-to-one tuition at home for certain subjects. She gave Mum a prospectus with her phone number on and told us to get in touch if I found anything I was interested in.

When we arrive back home I asked Dad to look through the prospectus with me to see what was on offer. (I must say now that although I had enjoyed my school days, with being so disabled I seemed to have spent more time on my therapy and not so much on the academic side and I had not done any exams at all). So when I saw a G.C.S.E. course in English I told Mum and Dad that I would like to try that. Dad said there was also one on money management which would be useful to me.

Mum said that she would phone and find out about the courses for me. The lady that we met on Saturday asked Mum to give her our phone number and she would arrange for one of the home tutors

P00EPL8U8

UNIVERSITY OF NOTTINGHAM

Routing
Sorting
Y02G09Z
Covering — BXXXX
Despatch

Ship To: 34752007 F

UNIVERSITY OF NOTTINGHAM
KINGS MEADOW CAMPUS
LENTON LANE
NOTTINGHAM
NOTTINGHAMSHIRE
NG7 2NA

Bill To: 34752007

UNIVERSITY OF NOTTINGHAM
KING'S MEADOW CAMPUS
LENTON LANE
NOTTINGHAM
NOTTINGHAMSHIRE
NG7 2NA

ISBN	Qty	Sales Order
1–904502–47–4	1	F 7284121 1

Customer P/O No Cust P/O List
DM1033 9.99 GBP

Fund: DERMED – 2006

Title: Giving life a go / by Ann Whitaker.

Format: Paperback
Author: Whitaker, Ann, 1964 –
Publisher: Best Books Online/Mediaworld PR
Volume:
Edition: **Year:** 2004

Order Specific Instructions

RUSH

to contact us. A few days later Mum had a phone call from Margaret Rolfe who said that she would call the following Thursday morning to have a chat about home tuition.

I was looking forward to finding out more about the courses. Mum made Margaret very welcome and she soon put me at my ease asking me questions about my schoolwork. I explained that I used a typewriter and that my speech was a little slow and hesitant, but Margaret said that was not a problem she would soon get used to me. She explained what a home tutor was then told me she would come one morning a week and together we would work our way through a normal school G.C.S.E. syllabus, setting me homework each week which she would mark. She also told me that we would work at my speed and it did not matter if it took two years to cover all the work, then she would enter me in that year's examinations.

Margaret told Mum that Monday morning was her only free time so it was arranged for her to come at 10.00 a.m. the last Monday in September. Also that this year they were running an extra class at Perins School on a Thursday evening; 'Maths for people with difficulties'. Mary, the tutor, could organise support workers if they were needed for anyone. Mum said, "I am sure Dad will take you to the maths class Ann, and you can see how you cope with that."

So that's what we agreed to do, I told Mrs Hancock that I would drop Mondays at the Hexagon Centre to concentrate on my English work with Margaret, and Dad said he would take me to my maths class on Thursday evenings.

The first Monday Margaret came, she asked me what books had I read, I told her, apart from my very early children's books, the only ones were the Katie books which I really enjoyed. I knew Mum had tried to get me interested in reading but I was not so keen, I would just glance through her magazines or look at the daily paper but that was all. Margaret said that she would look out one or two books for me to read then ask me questions afterwards to see how much I could remember.

This was the beginning of another wonderful friendship which is just as strong now, Margaret phones me every week to see how I am and also Mum and Dad. From the first time we met we just seemed to get on so well, I found that I could talk to Margaret about anything and I value her opinion and advice immensely.

When my Dad took me to the first Thursday evening maths class I was surprised to see such a wide range of ages in the group, from students who had just left school to elderly people in their sixties. Mary the tutor had two support workers with her and she asked Heather to sit with me and write for me as I cannot use a pen. This worked well in class, I would tell Heather what to write down, and for my homework I could do it in my own time on my typewriter. I soon settled into a routine, my Dad had put me a desk in the small bedroom and I could work on my own. I had my radio cassette player with me. Sometimes Mum would look in and say, "I don't know how you can work with that noise on all the time."

The maths class was based mainly on money management to help the group to get used to dealing with money and to budget their weekly allowances. Mary would explain to us about household accounts and that some bills are sent out quarterly, then get us to divide large amounts so we could see how much we needed each week, and also to be more economical when we were out shopping and compare prices.

Heather lived in Alresford and suggested that she could come and take me out shopping to help me get used to handling my own money. We had great fun going round the supermarket, I would put items in the trolley and Heather would look at me and ask "Are you sure you can afford that Ann? Remember you have only £10 to spend on food and that is to live on all the week." It certainly made me realise the value of money and to be more careful how I spent it.

When the weather was nice Dad and I would walk along the avenue to my maths class, we could see the river with the ducks and swans. Sometimes if we were lucky we would spot a Kingfisher hovering, then it would swoop down and catch a fish in its long beak.

During the following weeks Margaret brought me a number of books that she wanted me to read, one or two were children's books by Roald Dhal which I was not too keen on. Some of the others I found a little hard to get into and understand at first like 'Cider with Rosie' and others by Laurie Lee, also Karen Armstrong

'Through The Narrow Gate', but once I got into a book I found it easier and I persevered and then I enjoyed reading and wanted to know how the story ended.

Margaret would also ask me to write a short piece on different situations that I might find myself in. Like, being lost in a crowd, or to describe things you would see on a walk in the countryside. One that I found really hard was to make up a story using my imagination. It took me quite a while for me to make up a story with a beginning a middle and an ending. Margaret was a very good teacher and although she had to go over things and explain many times before I understood, she never got cross with me.

She would say, "Ann just try and think first and put yourself in the story and see how you would react". I must say that I found it hard work but I was also beginning to enjoy my English and I looked forward to Mondays with Margaret. After my lesson Mum would have coffee and biscuits ready for us and we would sit and chat about every day things. Margaret would tell us about her two sons, one was at Cambridge University and the other worked in a bank, and her husband who was the head of maths at Winchester College. Some days she would take us back to her house in Winchester for lunch.

Around this time a new couple moved into the bungalow next door to us, Daphne and Robin. They were in their late forties. Daphne worked in a shop in Winchester and Robin worked nights. He was such good fun, always telling jokes and teasing me, if I had my classical tapes on loud he would knock on my window and tell me to turn that rubbish off he was trying to sleep, but it was all in fun.

When he saw Mum getting my wheelchair out he would say, "if you are going to the Swan I will come with you and you can buy me a drink." Daphne was different, quiet and kept to herself, although she would talk to us if she saw us out in the garden. Robin would tease me about being from the north of England, I would tell him, "if you have never been to Blackpool you have not lived."

In the end he told me that they were going to Blackpool for a long weekend to see the illuminations, when they came back he had to agree that it was a wonderful sight and that he had really enjoyed the weekend. I don't think Daphne found it to her taste, she said it was too noisy and crowded for her liking.

When I attended one meeting of Faith and Light, Nancy told us about the annual pilgrimage to Walsingham being planned for September. This is one of the big events and groups from all over the country try to assemble together for this special day of prayer and thanksgiving. Helen had told me about Walsingham and said she hoped I could go with them. This year, Nancy told us, we are going to stay over night as she felt it was too much travelling there and back in one day and she was going to book rooms in a hotel for us all.

Back home, while we were having our Sunday tea, I told Mum and Dad about the weekend in Walsingham and asked if I could go with them. Mum said it would be good for me to be with my friends but first she would have to phone Nancy to see if they had enough help to cope with me. Nancy said they would love to take me and that Helen and Margaret could look after me, and we would all three share a room together. I was so excited and looking forward to the weekend.

Walsingham is a lovely old market town in Norfolk with narrow cobbled streets and old fashioned shops with bow windows, most of the churches are old except for a new Catholic church built in 1950. It is the place where it is said Our Blessed Lady appeared in the year 1061, a shrine was built there and over the years many kings and queens have visited the shrine to pray to Our Lady. For us today it is very popular and thousands of pilgrims visit to pray and to refresh themselves in the peace and quiet of this special place at the shrine of Our Lady. I suppose Walsingham is our own shrine, like Lourdes is to France.

The day arrived and Mum woke me early with a cup of tea as we were setting off from Winchester at 8.00 a.m. she had packed me an overnight bag and a packed lunch. I was excited about going with my new friends, and my parents were pleased that I was living a more normal kind of life. Dad took me into Winchester to meet my friends at St. Peter's Church, Nancy was organising everything and told Dad not to worry, she would keep an eye on me. Then Helen and Margaret arrived and helped me onto the coach, they said we like sitting at the back with all the young ones and have fun. John, the driver, soon had all the luggage packed away and told us we would stop for a short break and be in Walsingham by 1.00 p.m.

It was a beautiful morning the sun shone brightly and everyone was happy, we were singing along with the tape that John was playing and it did not seem long before he pulled into a service station and we stopped for our lunch break. Then off again and across country on our way to Norfolk and just on 1.00 p.m. we pulled into the car park, where there were about 30 coaches and crowds of people everywhere. At 1.30 p.m. we all gathered in the market place to say prayers before walking in procession the mile to the shrine of Our Lady, four men were carrying a large cross and some of the groups had their own banners with them. Then we had a wonderful Mass with beautiful singing and special prayers and blessings which the Holy Father had sent to be read out to us all.

After the Mass we had time to meet up with old friends again. I was pleased to see a group from the north and it was nice to chat about old times with them and catch up on all the news. Most of them were going straight back home after a meal so we stayed with them as we had time because Nancy had booked rooms for us in the town. As we watched them board the coaches ready for the journey home they were arranging to meet again at the Carol Service in London.

As we made our way back into the town centre Nancy told us that she had booked a meal for everyone at 6.30 p.m. so once she had shown us our rooms we were free to do as we liked. Margaret wanted to show me around the town but with the narrow streets, she found it hard pushing my wheelchair so we went in a café and had coffee then back to our hotel to freshen up before the evening meal. It was nice mixing with the group and getting to know them better, the meal was very good and by the time we had finished most of us felt tired but happy after a wonderful day. Helen and Margaret helped me to get ready for bed then made hot chocolate and we sat on our beds talking and having lots of fun.

Nancy had to wake us at 7.45 a.m. and told us not to forget and pack all our things before going down for breakfast, then Helen helped me to get dressed. I thanked them both for looking after me, they both said that it had been a pleasure I had not been any trouble. After breakfast we loaded up the coach and then made our way to church for morning Mass before setting off on our journey home. We were singing and having fun at the back of the bus when John said he had a surprise for us all, someone had arranged for us to stop for lunch on the way back and paid for it. Nancy said, "no, it is not me, it is from St. Peter's." One of the group then shouted three cheers for Nancy and St. Peter's and we all joined in.

Dad was waiting at the church when we arrived back, he thanked Nancy, Helen and Margaret for looking after me they all said that I had been no trouble and looked forward to the next trip. It was good to be home, I was tired but happy and it had been a wonderful experience for me I was soon in bed and slept twelve solid hours.

At the November meeting Nancy told us about the arrangements for the trip up to London on the second Saturday in December, some of the group in Eastleigh were coming with us on our coach and we would be leaving St. Peter's at 8.00 a.m. sharp. All the groups were meeting at Westminster Cathedral for midday Mass.

Dad took me into Winchester to meet my friends, it was a cold frosty morning and all the trees were white with frost and looked lovely. Nancy was there getting people onto the coach, Helen helped me on and we sat at the back, then Margaret came to sit with us. Once we were all on, John the driver told us we had to pick up our friends in Eastleigh then straight on to London.

It was about 11.30 a.m. as we pulled into the square by the Cathedral we could see other groups arriving and making their way inside, as we took our place I looked around and was amazed to see such a huge crowd of people. There were groups from all over England and colourful banners everywhere, as the Mass began and Cardinal Hume, the main celebrant, took his place, I felt in awe and privileged to be among so many people. The singing was joyful and uplifting and the Cardinal gave a lovely homily, then he blessed us all and said it was a pleasure for him to celebrate Mass for us.

After Mass we all went into the church hall and ate our packed lunch, Nancy came to our table and told Helen, as it was a fine day, if they wanted, they could walk to Trafalgar Square with me in my chair. We had to be there by 3.45 p.m. so that gave us two hours to look at the shops all decorated for Christmas, I had never been in London at this time of year before and seen so many people shopping. Margaret said we should go and have a hot drink but when we saw the prices we did not bother, but it was fun just being there and seeing the sights.

As we approached Trafalgar Square I was overwhelmed by the large crowd gathered there around the very tall Christmas tree, we made our way to where Nancy and the group were then all at once the Salvation Army band began playing the first carol. It was such a wonderful feeling to be there and the atmosphere so overwhelming it was another great moment in my life that I will always remember.

After the Carol Service we said our goodbyes to our friends then boarded the coach and John took us on a tour of the lights around London, it is a beautiful sight to see all the big stores decorated for Christmas. On the way home we stopped for fish and chips which we really did enjoy, arriving back in Winchester around 8.30 p.m. tired but very happy it had been a smashing day out.

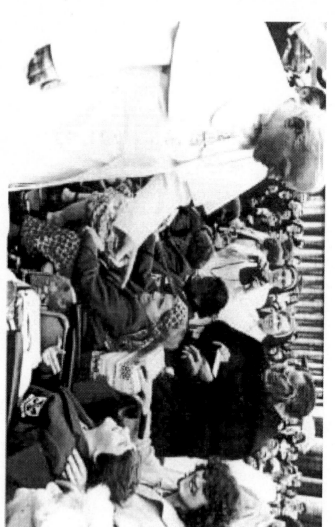

Ann with the Pope in 1978

Ann with Joan Young

Ann on her scooter

Ann with Mum and Dad

Ann as a guide

Ann on holiday with Mum

Chapter Twelve

There was a lovely couple who lived a little further along the Close, Lucy and Rob, they were in their late fifties. Rob was a master baker and would often call on his way home from work with a couple of cream cakes for Mum and me. Lucy was a very talented lady she painted wonderful landscape pictures and wrote poems and short stories for magazines. Once she had got to know me Lucy would call to see us and read my English homework, some times helping me or suggesting different ways to write a certain piece. Unfortunately Lucy had poor health, some days she could not do anything at all and Rob had to do everything for her, but they were a devoted couple and I still keep in touch with them.

One day while Lucy was at our house Mum mentioned that it would soon be my 21st birthday, nowadays 18 is the big coming-of-age day. Straight away Lucy said, "I will tell Rob and he will make Ann a birthday cake, it will be our pleasure."

I will always remember my 21st birthday it was on a Monday, poor Dad, he told us he was very sorry but it was the day of the Lord Mayor of London's annual visit and he would probably be working late. Mum was up early baking and making sandwiches, just before Dad left for work they came into my bedroom and both gave me a big kiss and wished me a happy birthday. Then Dad told me to put my arm out and he placed a beautiful gold watch on my wrist and said, "that is from us Ann, have a smashing day", he gave me a big hug then left for work.

Mum brought me a cup of tea and a huge pile of cards which she opened and read out to me, we counted up when she had finished and there was over fifty from my many friends and relations. She said; "it will be open house today Ann, I have pulled the table out and made a large trifle, plates of sandwiches, three dozen sausage rolls and fancy cakes so people can help themselves."

When I had been washed and dressed I went into the lounge and saw the table all set out with a beautiful birthday cake in the centre and all the food Mum had prepared, I was just amazed. Rob had decorated my cake with flowers in different colours and 'Happy 21st Birthday' in pink icing, it was so nice and it seemed a shame to cut into it.

Margaret came, gave me a hug and a gift, and said, "we are not doing any work today Ann, I am going to help your Mum, it will be a busy day for us all." People seemed to be popping in all the time, Nancy came with some friends from church and Lucy and other neighbours called, I thanked Lucy for the cake and said I would give Rob a big kiss when I saw him later. I received some lovely presents and it was good to see so many of my friends, by the time my Dad came home Mum and I were both tired out. He did offer to take us out for a meal but we said, "not tonight but you can on Friday night." He did and we had a real good meal.

Mum had invited Auntie Doris down for Christmas as we did not like her to be on her own. I was glad because we got on so well and we could spend most of the time together. She liked walking and would take me out into the countryside where we walked for miles. We talked about the many happy times we'd shared with Auntie Phyllis at their house when I used to stay for weekends. There was a bond between us that we both felt, she often said to me that if anything should happen to Mum and Dad she would be there to take care of me.

We all enjoyed Christmas together, Dad took us to the Carol Service in Winchester Cathedral two days before Christmas. The singing was wonderful I could see Auntie Doris enjoyed it, she was joining in all the carols. The cathedral was packed, people were standing down the side and at the back.

On Christmas Eve we all walked to Midnight Mass in Alresford, it was a clear frosty night with the sky full of stars. As we sang the opening carol the altar boys walked down the aisle, followed by Father Spencer, to the crib where he laid baby Jesus in the manger. For me that is what Christmas really means, to remember the birthday of Jesus Christ. After Mass we made our way home and had a hot drink then opened our Christmas presents before going to bed.

Mum did us proud with a smashing Christmas lunch which we all enjoyed. Auntie Doris took me for a walk while Dad washed the dishes and Mum had a well deserved rest. On Boxing Day Dad took us to the pantomime in Southampton, Les Dawson was the star in *'Jack and the Bean Stalk'*, it was a really good show and everyone enjoyed it. Auntie Doris was singing in *'The Messiah'* so she could not stay over the New Year. Before she returned home, she asked Dad if he would help her organise a surprise birthday party for my Grandad. He would be eighty years old and she wanted to make it a special day for him, as it would be the Easter weekend she asked us all to come and stay with her for the holiday. Dad said that he would help her with the party and make it extra special for him.

Early in the New Year when Elizabeth came to give me my physiotherapy she said, "Ann you are getting really good at your exercises now, I think that I have done all the physio' I can. What you need now is to learn how to relax your body more, I think I have just the right man who can help you. His name is Bob Donavan, he is an American and he teaches the Alexander Technique, I know you will like him."

Mum was very interested and asked Elizabeth for Bob's phone number so we could contact him to arrange an appointment. My Dad phoned Bob and he said he would come and see us on Saturday morning to explain about the treatment.

When Bob arrived I felt very nervous but he soon put me at ease, he was such a kind gentleman. He asked me about my disability and what treatment I'd had, I told him that from a very early age I'd had physiotherapy, horse riding and swimming. While I was talking I could see Bob watching me, he said, "are you always so tense Ann?" I said I was, and that sometimes it was very embarrassing for me.

"Well Ann," he said, "the main aim of my treatment is to try and relax your muscles and use your body properly. If your Dad will bring you to my house in Winchester on Friday evening we will see how things work out. I am sure with your determination it will."

It took me quite a while to realise what Bob wanted me to do. In the centre of his treatment room he had a large table with a soft cover. I had to lie down and he raised my head on some books so it was just above my body, then he asked me to relax all my body starting with my feet and working up to my head.

Then he did some bending and stretching movements with my legs, talking quietly all the time. Next he had me walking around the room in my bare feet while he just held my head straight. He asked me if I could feel any sensation through my body and I told him no. "Don't worry Ann," he said, "you will and then you will know things are working." He told me to do the stretching exercise at home and also to stand against the wall and slide my body down as I bent my knees.

I felt really tired after my session with Bob but, as with all my treatment over the years, I knew it was for my own good and I put every effort into it. Mum always felt sorry for me when she saw me like that, but Bob told her it would get easier and wanted me to come every other Friday. It took me about two months to learn what Bob was teaching me, then one evening when Bob was working on my shoulders I felt a tingling sensation pass down my body I looked up at Bob and he smiled at me, he knew what had happened and said, "that is what I have been waiting for Ann."

Bob told us that he treats many professional people how to relax properly and control their movements. "Just because you are disabled Ann," he said, "does not mean you should be disadvantaged." Both Bob and his wife Barbara are very caring people, even now, though they have moved to live in France, we still write to each other.

As it got nearer to Easter Dad seemed to be on the phone with Auntie Doris more and more, organising Grandad's birthday party. He liked to go to the 'Brown Cow' in Bingley and she had booked a private room for Sunday lunch. Doris told Dad that she had talked to his brother and three sisters and they said that they would be there with their families.

We travelled up on Good Friday and we called to see Grandad first. Dad said, "we are going to take you out for lunch on Sunday as a birthday treat and will call for you at midday". I asked Grandad if there was anything special he would like for his birthday and he said, "at my age there is not much I need, but I would like to see Morecambe again, it has always been my favourite resort."

When we got back in the car I asked Dad if he could hire a mini bus for the day to take Grandad and some relations to Morecambe? He said when we get to Doris' he would look in the local paper and see what he could do.

Auntie Doris was pleased to see us again and had a lovely meal ready for us. Dad mentioned about hiring a mini-bus for the day and she though it was a good idea. He looked in the paper and found a local firm and booked a bus for Monday. Auntie asked me if I would like to go with her to a concert at Chapel on Saturday, I said I would like that and it would be lovely to see some of my friends again.

Dad said he would go down to 'The Brown Cow' and make sure everything was arranged for the party. Auntie told him that everyone knew to be there for 12 o'clock, and she would be there and keep them in the restaurant so it would be a wonderful surprise when Grandad walked through the door.

Sunday morning arrived and Dad took me to early Mass at St. Anne's in Keighley, that is the church Grandad Bob attended, and where he often took me when I was very young. It brought back a lot of happy memories for me and I felt a bit sad as I sat in church and just wondered what Bob would say if he could see me now, all grown up.

We called for Grandad and he asked where we were going but I just said, "It is a birthday surprise, but I am sure you will enjoy it", then we drove off to 'The Brown Cow'. It certainly was a surprise when Grandad walked into the restaurant, there were about thirty people and they all shouted "Happy Birthday Richard". Even I was amazed how many relations were there, including Uncle Ken from Manchester, (who is my favourite uncle). I don't think Grandad could believe his eyes as he looked around and saw everyone.

Grandad's favourite meal is roast beef with Yorkshire pudding and here they serve it the proper way, the Yorkshire pudding first, on its own. When the waiter served the puddings I was amazed at the size, they filled the dinner plate and came with lovely onion gravy, it was delicious, I had never seen any as big before. The tender roast beef, came with roast potatoes, carrots, sprouts and horseradish sauce. Then we had sherry trifle to finish, and real champagne for the toast.

I think everyone was so full we just sat around talking and enjoying ourselves. Grandad was overwhelmed by it all, but I could see that he was pleased to see everyone there. It was good to see my relations, some I had not seen for a long time with moving down south.

Around three o'clock the waiters served coffee and biscuits before the guests started making their way home. During the meal my Dad asked Auntie Florence and Annie if they would like to come to Morecambe with us, they both said they would love to so we would have a full mini bus.

We took Grandad back to his flat and stayed with him, looking at his many birthday cards, while Mum helped Auntie Doris make tea but none of us were very hungry. Before we left, Dad said, "we will call for you at eleven o'clock tomorrow and take you out for the day." I gave Grandad a big hug and told him to have an early night, then he would enjoy his day out, we left and went back to Auntie's house. Dad thanked her for arranging everything and we all agreed that it had been a wonderful success and a day Grandad would remember.

Next morning Dad went to the garage to collect the mini bus, then called for Auntie Annie and Auntie Florence before coming back for us. Auntie Doris was waiting at the entrance with Grandad, she had arranged to borrow a wheelchair from the warden at his flats so he would not get too tired walking all day.

It was a lovely sunny morning as we left Bingley, my Dad said, "I think I will go straight to Morecambe this morning, then coming home, we can take the scenic route". The roads were not too busy and in no time at all we pulled into a car park in the centre of Morecambe.

"I think we should have something to eat first," said Mum, "and then do whatever Grandad wants in the afternoon".

So we found a nice café and we all had a lovely meal, Mum and Grandad both love fish and chips so they had that. As soon as he tasted it, he said; "this is a jumbo haddock you can tell the difference with the big white flakes."

I had not been to Morecambe for many years and it was nice to walk on the promenade and the pier. Auntie Florence was telling me about when my Dad was a little boy and one holiday in Morecambe he pushed Auntie Doris over the railings into the sea.

Grandad and another man had to jump in and pull her out quickly because the tide was on the turn and she could have been washed away. She said Doris was screaming her head off, but was more upset because she had lost a brand new bonnet. I bet my Dad got into trouble when they got back to the guest house where they were staying. Auntie said in those days the whole Whitaker clan came to Morecambe every year in the Bingley holiday week. She said all the mills closed down and the town was deserted, people either went to Blackpool, Morecambe or Scarborough.

Auntie Annie told us that they had built a new promenade from the 'Battery' along the seafront to Heysham Head. "I know Richard always liked going up to Heysham," she said, "we used to all take a picnic and meet Agnes and Edgar with their family from Manchester."

We had a lovely walk along the seafront. Doris was pushing Grandad and Dad pushed me, the sun was out and you could see for miles, right across Morecambe Bay to Grange-Over-Sands with the Cumbrian fells in the far distance. Grandad said, "Just breath in that fresh air Ann, it is better than a bottle of medicine, you don't need to go abroad for holidays we have it all here."

We then made our way up into the village and had afternoon tea in one of the little tea shops which are so quaint. Afterwards we walked by the Strawberry Gardens and back into Morecambe and to the car park ready to make our way home.

We travelled back over The Trough of Bowland where the views are wonderful, you can see right over the Yorkshire Dales to Ingleborough, and the other way all along the Lancashire coast line, then on through Gisburn and Skipton and back to Bingley.

Grandad told us he had a wonderful day out and it brought back many happy memories for him. He thanked Dad for taking them and for giving him a lovely weekend.

Next day Mum took Auntie Doris shopping to Leeds by train and Dad took me to see some of my friends in Keighley where we used to live then the following day we returned home.

Not long after Grandad's birthday we had been to 11 o'clock Mass and, as usual Dad got 'The Universe' which is a Catholic newspaper. After Sunday lunch as I looked through the paper I saw advertised a pilgrimage for Hosanna House, Lourdes in August. I asked Mum and Dad if I could go, they said I could, so I wrote for details. When I received the itinerary and list of passengers I looked to see if there was anyone I knew, the name Sister Felicity rang a bell with me as I had a housemother at St. Rose's called Felicity and I wondered if it was the same person.

I remembered reading about Hosanna House a couple of years earlier, when they were fund raising to buy a property on the outskirts of Lourdes where groups of pilgrims could stay for a week. It would be staffed by the Sisters and have trained medical people on duty 24 hours a day. They would also have their own special buses to take the pilgrims into the Domain. One of the reasons why I wanted to join a group was that each disabled person had their own helper for the week, so I knew that I would be well cared for and could go on my own. The groups are made up of a leader, a priest and a nurse, some may have a doctor if any seriously ill pilgrims are included in the party.

We were flying out from Gatwick Airport and had to be there for three o'clock Friday afternoon. Dad said, "that's alright Ann we will take you then go on to Eastbourne for a few days holiday, it will be a nice break for us".

As soon as we entered the departure lounge I spotted a man holding a banner proclaiming 'Hosanna House', so we made our way over to him. He introduced himself and told me he was Pat Porter the group leader, then asked me my name. I told him and after looking at his list he said, "right Ann, your helper for the week is Sister Jane, she has not arrived yet but there is plenty of time". He then gave me my name badge and told me to wear it all the time. Pat was about fifty with black hair, spectacles and was always smiling. His wife was tall and slim, I thought she looked like a teacher I knew.

Pat told Dad what he liked about the pilgrimages was that he got sent a list of people and usually didn't know anyone, but by the end of the week everyone was friends and you would think they had known each other for ages.

Mum and Dad gave me a big hug and a kiss and told me to have a lovely time. Pat said, "don't worry about Ann, I am sure she will be alright and I will keep an eye on her". Then they left us and set off to Eastbourne, I was happy that they were having a break on their own while I was away.

Soon more people were arriving, I was glad that there were some about my age and I was looking forward to the week in Lourdes. Then a tall blonde lady came up to me and said, "Hi Ann, I am Sister Jane." What a surprise! She was in ordinary clothes and I could tell by her accent that she was American. I had been used to seeing nuns at St. Rose's and in church but they always wore their habit, it seemed strange to see Sister Jane dressed just like us apart from a cross around her neck. She gave me a big hug and said, "We are bed mates for the week, you will have to tell me what help you need, I am sure we will have great fun."

Then it was time to board the plane and begin our journey to Lourdes.

As quite a number of our party were in wheelchairs, we were the first passengers to board and could choose the best seats. Sister Jane helped me on to the plane and let me sit by the window, she was very friendly and so easy to talk to. She told me most Sisters in America wear day clothes unless they are in an enclosed order. She asked me if I had been to Lourdes before?

"Yes this will be my fourth pilgrimage".

"That is good Ann," she said, "because I have never been, so you can be my guide this week."

Then she told me that when she returned home she was being sent out to the Cameroon with two more Sisters to work in a Mission School, she was really looking forward to that. It seemed no time at all before we were coming into land at Tarbes Airport which is about twelve miles from Lourdes.

Coaches were waiting to take the passengers to their hotels. Pat soon had our group organised and on our way to Hosanna House.

The Sisters had a meal ready for us as soon as we arrived, which was very welcome. Sister Jane could speak French quite well and kept trying to teach me the odd word. While we ate our meal Pat came to each table and gave us our room numbers, then told us that a bus would be leaving at eight o'clock if anyone wanted to go to the grotto to say the Rosary.

After the meal we went to our room and unpacked, we were on the first floor and from the window there was a lovely view right across the valley with the high mountains of the Pyrenees in the far distance. One of the Sisters then came to our room to ask if there was anything we may need, Sister Jane asked her about the house. She told us that the house used to be a Convent but the Sisters moved out a few years ago. Now after much alteration it was used by the Trust for groups to stay for a week. The idea was that each party would do as much as possible for themselves, the Sisters cooked lunch and an evening meal and there was a kitchenette that visitors could use to make a drink and snacks. Also there was a beautiful chapel on the ground floor that we were welcome to use.

Sister Jane asked me if I felt like going out because she was eager to see the grotto where Bernadette had first seen the apparition of Our Lady, I said, "Yes please but we must take a coat with us because it can get chilly at night". We then went downstairs to wait for the bus to take us down to the Domain, this was the first time we had really got to meet the other members of our party. There was a young family with a girl who was about six years old called Beth. She looked very ill and her mum told us that she had leukaemia. (I heard later that she had died).

Then another nun came across to meet us, she was a large old Sister dressed in the black habit with her dress down to the floor and a heavy veil, she told us she was Sister Felicity, a Carmelite from the Notting Hill Monastery in London. I realised then that it was not the same person who was at St. Rose's when I was there. As I got to know her she told me that she did not agree with nuns wearing day clothes, and said things were changing too quickly in the world.

This was another person who I became very good friends with. When I lived down south my parents used to take me to see her and now I write or phone her regularly. She listens to me and when I have asked, she has always given me good advice.

We then loaded the buses and the drivers took us into Lourdes, Pat told us to be at St. Michael's gate for 10.00 p.m. and not to be late. As we walked down the avenue we could hear the people singing the 'Ave' which is Our Lady's hymn. At the corner, as we looked into the main square, the crowd was enormous. Sister Felicity who was with us said it would be very busy this week because Wednesday was the Feast of the Assumption of Our Blessed Lady, and we would be taking part in all the processions and ceremonies. Sister Jane whispered in my ear, "we shall be holy all day". We then made our way to the grotto and said the rosary with the rest of our group, then we walked through the town and had a night cap before joining the bus for home.

At breakfast next morning Pat told us that Father Michael would be saying Mass in the house chapel at ten o'clock, then we were free until two o'clock when we were joining the Blessed Sacrament Procession.

I asked Sister Jane if she would like to walk and see the sheep fold in Bartres where Bernadette lived after she had seen the apparitions and before being accepted into the Convent. It was a lovely sunny morning as we walked slowly down, I showed Sister the sheep hut and the little church where she made her First Holy Communion.

We then had morning coffee and a cream cake at a wayside café before making our way back, it was so peaceful in the countryside. As we reached the top of the hill we sat and looked across the valley, you could just hear the bells of the Basilica in the far distance and I felt as if I was in another world.

In the afternoon we took the bus into Lourdes and joined the other pilgrims in Rosary Square for the Procession of the Blessed Sacrament. This is a special service for the very sick pilgrims who stay in the hospital just by the Domain. They are brought out in their wheelchairs to receive a blessing. The bishop walks down each row holding the Blessed Sacrament high, giving a blessing to everyone. Prayers are said and hymns sung throughout the service, it is a very emotional experience seeing so many people who are much worse off than ourselves.

As we left the square after the service Sister Jane said, "Ann that is one of the most moving times that I have ever experienced, it makes one feel so humble, seeing all those sick patients". We were very quiet as we made our way back to the bus and home.

During supper, Sister Felicity said that she had spoken to the sister-in-charge and asked if we could join the sisters in morning prayer. She said we could and told us that they have Mass at 7.00 a.m., each morning and we would be most welcome. "No more lying in now Ann," whispered Sister Jane.

That evening we all went to the Torchlight Procession. The guides were organising everyone into lines, there were thousands of people there, then as the bells of the Basilica struck eight we all lit our candles and sung the hymn *Immaculate Mary*. We walked all along the river bank, past the grotto, up one side of the avenue and down the other, round Our Lady's statue into Rosary Square and lined up in front of the Basilica to say the rosary together. Although you are among crowds of people all these ceremonies seem so very personal to you.

The following day, Father Michael had arranged for us to have Mass said at the grotto. This is always very difficult to organise because that is the place where Bernadette saw the eighteen apparitions and is a Holy Shrine. Every group tries to have a Mass there, but unlike the Basilicas and other churches, which can hold hundreds of people, at the grotto just a small area is cordoned off and it is not unusual to see Mass being said from seven in the morning until midday.

We would be joined by another English group with two bishops and four priests, including our own, celebrating Mass. As I looked into the grotto, which is a cave cut into the hillside, behind the altar is a statue of Our Blessed Lady dressed in white holding her rosary. Just looking up at that statue, and thinking about all the millions of people who go each year to Lourdes, made me think what a miraculous event had taken place when a young girl saw a vision all those years ago. It was a beautiful Mass and I always feel so emotional sat by the grotto in these quiet, peaceful surroundings.

I asked Sister Jane what were her thoughts and she just said,

"Ann, I looked at you and the others around us and I'm so happy to be here. People have told me to visit Lourdes many times and I wondered what they meant, but I now know". We then walked on by the river and talked for a while before going home for lunch.

That afternoon we just sat in the grounds relaxing in the peaceful surroundings. Pat and his wife came across and asked us if we would like to take a packed lunch next day, then after we'd done the Stations, we could walk up to the picnic area there. We all agreed that it was a good idea.

In the evening we went down to the Domain, Sister Felicity said, "If we walk up the road, just past St. Michael's gate we can have a good view of the Torchlight Procession".

It really is an impressive scene to see hundreds of people walking, each one holding a lighted candle, going all around the Domain singing hymns and saying prayers.

After the procession we went down to the grotto and sat there in the quietness each with our own thoughts. Sister Felicity turned to me and said, "these are precious moments in our lives that we must treasure, think of them as the Miracle of Lourdes".

She told me people came there, not expecting physical miracles, although some do happen, but to reflect on their lives, take stock, recharge their batteries with God's graces so as to be able to carry on. Sister was a very holy person but also worldly, she talked to me a lot that week.

Next morning we were up early saying prayers with the Sisters before breakfast. Pat had organised a packed lunch for us, and the buses took us into Lourdes. Then we walked up the hillside to begin saying the Stations of the Cross. You see the fourteen Stations in all Catholic Churches spaced around the walls depicting the last journey that Our Lord made to Calvary. Here the Stations are about fifteen feet tall and look so commanding as they stand on the hillside. As we approached each Station, Father Michael led us through the special prayers that follow Christ's footsteps on his way to his crucifixion. This was a very moving experience, seeing Christ nailed to the cross in such surroundings made me realise the enormity of it all.

Higher up the hillside a picnic area has been made, there were wooden tables and benches and also some tree trunks to sit on. As we ate our lunch and looked at the breathtaking view across the valley we could see the cable cars and the railway making its way up the mountain. Pat then told us we were free for the rest of the day, but the bus would take anyone out if they wanted.

I asked Sister Jane if she would mind taking me to the baths? Of course she said yes and asked me about them. I told her that the baths were filled from the spring that Bernadette had found when Our Lady told her to dig in the ground near the grotto, and it never stopped running. People believe the water has healing qualities and that is why they take the baths.

As you enter a lady is there to help you undress and put a robe around you, then you move to where the large stone baths are filled with the running waters from the spring. With someone holding you at each side you are placed into the bath and totally submerged, lifted out and the robe placed back on and you get dressed again. What always amazes me is, as soon as they lift you out of the bath, you are completely dry and I don't know how this can be. Prayers are being said all the time, both inside the baths and by the people outside waiting to go in.

Just a little way along past the baths are the large iron stands that hold dozens of candles, you can buy candles of all sizes, some are about four feet long. It is a full time job for the men there, as soon as one frame is empty they fill it again, you can see candles burning day and night. Many pilgrims come down to the grotto during the night when it is quiet and just sit and pray.

At supper Pat told us that as tomorrow was the 15th August and the Feast of the Assumption, many coaches would be bringing even more people in for this special feast day, so we would have to make an early start and be down at the Basilica before 8.00 a.m., breakfast would be from 6.30 and we were to leave at 7.30 a.m. After supper, Sister Jane said, "tomorrow is going to be a hard day for everyone, so I think we should both have an early night tonight".

We were all up early, breakfast finished and were ready to get on the buses by 7.30 a.m. Even so when we arrived at St. Joseph's gate I was surprised to see so many people around. The special Mass would be held in the underground Basilica, this is the largest church in Lourdes and can hold over twenty five thousand. Pat said it would take a long time to get everyone in so we would have to be patient. The underground Basilica is so different to any I have seen, the altar is on a raised platform in the centre of this large oval shaped building. Father Michael would be one of the fifty or so bishops and priests celebrating this Mass. I will never forget how I felt when the great organ started playing and the long procession of altar boys, bishops and priests made their way to the high altar and the congregation sang the opening hymn.

This was a sung High Mass celebrating the reception of Our Lady into heaven and with so many people there the atmosphere was electric. At communion the priests went to different areas in the church, but even then it took quite a long time for everyone to take part and I was surprised when Sister told me that it was eleven o'clock as Mass ended.

By the time we had made our way out of the Basilica Pat told us the bus would take us back home. Sister Jane asked me if I would like to stay in town and have lunch with her as we had to be in the square again by 2.00 p.m. for the Blessing of the sick. We made our way into the town and sat outside a café and had a sandwich and lovely cream cakes with delicious coffee to follow. We then looked around the shops before making our way into the Domain and sat by the river to relax in the pleasant sunshine for a while.

When the bells began ringing we made our way into the square and found a cool spot under the trees at one side of the square and watched all the sick pilgrims being wheeled across from the hospital. A new hospital has now been built which opened in 1997 there are two chapels and 1,300 beds.

The procession of the Blessed Sacrament is a special service for all the sick pilgrims in Lourdes and takes place each afternoon. If the weather is too wet, it takes place in the underground Basilica, prayers are said and hymns sung throughout this service which puts the less fortunate at the centre to receive God's Blessings.

I felt ready for my evening meal which we all enjoyed, Sister Felicity told me to have a rest on my bed for an hour as we would be out again for the Torchlight Procession at 8.00 p.m. As we were waiting for the buses to take us into the Domain, Pat said, "tomorrow is our last full day, so after we have Mass in the small chapel by Rosary Square, the rest of the day is free, but don't forget the fancy dress party in the evening".

The Torchlight Procession is so massive there are thousands of people each holding a lighted candle as they walk up one side of the long boulevard and down the other then assemble in Rosary Square. All the time prayers are said and hymns sung in so many different languages but each with the same meaning. It was a beautiful ending to a most wonderful day, although I felt tired and it had been a long day, inside I felt refreshed and so uplifted it was hard to explain. Sister Jane said in our room that night that she'd had many different emotions while being prepared to take her vows, but this week has been one of the most moving in all her life and, she continued, "it has been my pleasure to share it with you Ann."

It seemed no time at all before I was being woken with a cup of tea by one of the nuns to see if I wanted to go to morning prayers with them. Even that simple service made me feel part of them, although I could not understand all their prayers, I said my own silent ones.

After breakfast the buses took us into Lourdes and Father Michael lead us through a simple thanksgiving Mass in the side chapel of the Basilica. He asked us to pray for all our friends and relations and any special intentions of our own.

After our Mass we had a group photograph taken in front of the statue of Our Lady in Rosary Square. Sister Felicity said she was going to sit by the grotto for a while. I asked Sister Jane if she would take me around the shops as I wanted to buy one or two presents to take home with me. While we were in the shops Sister Jane suggested we buy some sandwiches and drinks and have a picnic lunch. "Yes," I said, "let's sit on the Prarie." This is open ground on the other side of the river opposite the grotto. So we went back to the grotto to find Sister Felicity then went over the bridge and sat with some others from our group and just relaxed for a while.

It is so restful there, although there are people in the distance somehow you don't seem to notice them. Looking at the grotto with the statue of Our Lady and the great Basilica in the background, I thought back to how it was over a hundred years ago when a young girl went to pick firewood and saw the vision of a lady who told her to pray. How would she feel now if she could see Lourdes today where every year over six million pilgrims come just to pray.

We then made our way to St. Michael's gate and the bus home. During our meal Pat said he had brought the boxes down so we could dress up for our party night. John could play the piano so we had a good sing, Bill had done a collection and bought some bottles of wine and a few nibbles and everybody had an enjoyable time.

During the party Pat told us Father Michael would be saying Mass at 8.00 a.m. in the chapel, then if anyone wanted to go to the grotto the bus would leave at 9.00 a.m. but only for one hour, as the coach would be coming at 11.30 a.m. to take us to the airport. He said we must pack and clear our rooms before going out, so that the Sisters could clean and get ready for the next group.

Sister Jane said she wanted to go to the grotto one more time before we left and asked me to go with her. We sat for a while, each with our own thoughts, then I said when I came here with a group from school Father Hinchcliffe showed me a mark on the ground just near Bernadette's statue. He told us all if we knelt down and touched that spot we would be sure to return, I said I always touched it and knew in my heart that I would return. We then had to go back in the bus and just had time for a drink before the coach came to take us to the airport.

Luckily there wasn't much of a delay before we boarded and were soon on our way home. Dad had told me he would be waiting at Gatwick for me and I was looking forward to introducing my new friends. When we landed Pat was told that we would be taken straight through customs to one of the private lounges where we would be checked out, then we could go. I saw Mum and Dad among the group of people waiting in the lounge and waved to them. When they came over, I introduced Sister Jane and she told them it had been a wonderful week and her pleasure and privilege to be my helper, we had lots of fun as well as some very moving moments. She told Mum that I was a very special girl that took her religion seriously.

Mum thanked them for looking after me, Sister Jane gave me a big hug and said she would always remember this week. Dad thanked Pat then I said my goodbyes and we left for home.

I had so much to tell my parents about my pilgrimage in Lourdes, sharing all the special celebrations and services with our group together. I told them how different Sister Jane and Sister Felicity were, although both were very devout, Sister Jane was more open and down to earth. Mum said that is partly due to the different order that they belonged to, most Carmelites are in enclosed orders and when Sister Felicity joined they had very strict rules and it was a hard life. I said although I enjoyed going around with Sister Jane, there was a deeper feeling for Sister Felicity I listened and tried to understand what she told me.

Chapter Thirteen

I soon settled back at the Hexagon Centre, two new clients had started while I was away Pamela and Steven. Pamela was a very quiet person in a wheelchair and came into our section to do typing and craft, she told me she lived in Romsey and her father was a vicar there. We became good friends and would sit and talk at lunchtime. Her mother had died the previous year and now her auntie was housekeeper at the vicarage. I told her about being at St. Rose's and Newhaven, then she surprised me by telling me that she had been at Trelores for four years and knew my Dad. Pam had been in the same house where my Dad was housemaster and had also done woodwork and craft, she said that he was a good teacher all the children liked him.

Steven was a very noisy boy, he came to try typing but did not like it much so he went to do woodwork and gardening. Steven had also been at Trelores and teased me about my dad.

Early in November Mum and I were invited on a weekend retreat at Park Place Pastoral Centre. During lunch on the first day we were sat with some ladies from the cathedral in Portsmouth when Sister Evelyn came across to introduce us. One of the ladies, Paula, told me that she was the youth team leader for our area and the bishop was moving her office and also the bookshop to Park Place in January. As Mum heard this she said, "maybe Ann you could do some voluntary work for them when they are settled in?"

This was another change of direction for me, and a chance of making more friends. Paula phoned Mum at the end of January and asked if she could come to see us about me helping one day a week at Park Place. Of course Mum and I were delighted, I have always wanted to do something with my life, maybe this was the beginning for me. We decided that I would go for the day every Tuesday. Mum would ask Dial-A-Ride to take me, a nice lady called Jackie took me in the morning, she was full of fun, and Dad would collect me on his way home from college at night.

Paula is a lovely lady she lives in Portsmouth and as well as running the youth group she organises the annual trip to Lourdes for the Handicapped Children's Pilgrimage Trust (H.C.P.T.). This takes place every Easter when thousands of disabled children and helpers spend a week together in Lourdes.

I soon got used to the routine. When Dad had gone to work at 8.00a.m., Mum helped me to get ready and also made a packed lunch for me to take, then off in the bus to Park Place. Julie, who worked in the office with Paula and was about my age, always had a coffee ready for me as soon as I arrived. We got on well together while she was typing the letters I had a list of addresses to type then stick the labels on the envelopes.

Julie also brought sandwiches and we sat together for lunch and talked about all kinds of things. If it was a nice day we sat outside or Julie would take me for a walk around the grounds. Some days I never saw Paula at all because she was out at a meeting around the diocese.

After lunch I went into the bookshop to help Meg there. She was a tall, dark-haired lady who I knew by sight as she and her family attended our church in Alresford. Meg showed me where the different books were on the shelves, if there had been a delivery I had to check each book against the invoice and make sure everything was all right. Sometimes I helped the customers if they were looking for a special book, I enjoyed meeting people and they got used to me.

What I most looked forward to was going into the chapel for afternoon prayers with the Sisters. Then one of the Sisters would make me a cup of tea and we would sit and talk, they were so interesting telling me about their lives in India and all the different places they had been.

Dad would arrive about five fifteen to take me home, I would be sat in the entrance hall waiting. There was always so much to tell Mum and Dad while we had our evening meal together, although I was tired when I got home, I felt that I had done something useful with my day and I did enjoy my work.

The following week at Park Place Julie was writing out a programme for the Annual Youth Day. This year it was going to take place in Basingstoke. This is an event for all the diocese and different parishes take turns in organising it, both able and disabled people join in and every one has a really good time. Julie asked me if I was going and I told her that I would be there with the Winchester group. Nancy is the leader and we have a very good crowd of young helpers who also join in, it is a real fun day on the Saturday and we all usually end up getting wet through with the water games.

Then we have a lovely Mass in the open air with lots of joyful hymns, some time the bishop will be the main celebrant if he is free. After Mass there is a barbecue for everybody and a sing-song before we go home, tired but happy. I love to see all the people mix together and joining in, also it is nice to see friends again you may only meet once a year.

I had quite a varied life now living at home, going to the Hexagon Centre three days a week, Park Place every Tuesday, the hydrotherapy on Thursday mornings and out with Mum in the afternoons. I had made friends at the monthly meetings of Faith and Light in Winchester where I enjoyed the outings and holidays that Nancy arranged for us all.

In Dad's summer holidays he would take us out for the day, we were lucky, living so near the South coast, and could be in Lee-On-Solent in half an hour. I loved to watch the big liners going into Southampton and the oil tankers to the depot off Fawley. Across the Solent is the Isle of Wight with the ferry and hovercraft and always yachts sailing by.

I remember one time Dad took me to see the 'Tall Ships', we saw it on the local T.V. news and Dad asked me if I would like to go and see them. Mum told us to go on our own as she was not so interested and said we could be waiting around a long time to see them.

What a magnificent sight watching them sail down Southampton Water and out into the Solent, it seemed to take hours for them all to pass by. There were ships from all over the world, each flying their national flag with lovely coloured sails. I had never seen sailing ships before, only small yachts. There were crowds of people lining the seafront to see them pass, all waving and cheering.

Sometimes we would go to Bournmouth and call and see Father Spencer, he had been our priest in Alresford before being moved to

Bournmouth. He still kept in touch and often called to see us when on his way back from London where he did quite a lot of legal work for the church. He had trained as a lawyer and worked in Rome for a few years before being sent back to the Portsmouth diocese. He told us anytime we were in Bournmouth to call on him.

A couple of months after I came back from Lourdes I had a letter and some photographs from Sister Felicity in London. She had been telling all the Sisters about me and Mother Superior wanted to meet me. Sister had written directions for my Dad and the phone number so he could arrange when to go. We were all a bit anxious about going to the monastery and did not know what to expect as they are an enclosed order and do not have much contact with the outside world. Sister Felicity is like their housekeeper and lives on her own in the courtyard entrance, she does the shopping, looks after visitors and also the sacristy.

Dad followed Sister's directions through London to Notting Hill where the Monastery is. As we turned into St. Charles Square and saw the high wall and big closed gate Mum said to me, "Ann we have been all over visiting friends you have made, but this looks daunting."

My Dad rang the bell by the gate and we could hear someone unlock it then Sister Felicity appeared, welcomed us and took us into her parlour as she called it. Everywhere was so spartan, plain wooden chairs to sit on, no floor covering, all the woodwork painted dark brown and white painted walls.

There were two telephones on a side table by another door, Sister told me that the red phone was for her to contact the Sisters inside. At meal times they would ring and a Sister would pass her meal through the door. She had a small kitchenette where she could make a drink and a snack, she made us a drink of tea and explained, even though she was of the same order, she could not mix with the other Sisters and said, "only when I stop working out here and put on the brown habit will I be allowed inside."

After a drink and a chat Sister said, "I will ring Mother and let her know you are here then she will arrange to meet you".

While Sister was on the phone Mum said to me, "Ann what are

we doing here? It's like medieval times and a bit frightening".

Sister said, "Mother will see you now and the bell will ring when she is ready". Then she took us out into the passage into a small waiting room. In a while a bell rang and we went into another small room. It was very bare, no windows and only a low light shining. At the far end there was a metal grill and, at the other side, I could just make out two shapes.

Sister Felicity took us forward and introduced us and told us to sit down then left. Mother Superior was a very small person with a quiet gentle voice. She said, "this is Sister Mary with me," then she asked me about myself and what I did. She seemed very interested in what I said then, after about fifteen minutes, she pressed a bell and Sister Felicity came back into the room. Mother then gave us a blessing and a screen was closed across the grill and we went back into the parlour.

We stayed talking to Sister for quite a while then she took us across the courtyard to the church. Sister said she looked after the church with the help of another lady as it was open to the parish for Mass. As I looked at the altar I could see a separate section to one side, Sister told me that was where the nuns sat so that the congregation could not see them. It all seemed so strange to me and I did not understand the order at all. I have met many nuns, mostly teaching or nursing sisters, and could understand their way of life, but all this was different. Sister told us that theirs is a life of prayer with only a small time spent in work, making altar breads and vestments for the church. We then said our goodbyes and left for home.

Mum told Dad to find somewhere to stop for refreshments and get back into the normal world. She said, "it is not that I don't like Sister Felicity, she is very worldly and a kind person, but I don't understand people wanting to live that life now. I am sure they could do just as much and be part of the community."

We often talked about our first visit to see Sister, we used to go about three times a year and in the summer she came to stay in their house in Bournmouth for a fortnight and we went down there to see her. She stayed with Sister Mary, their housekeeper, who had a cottage next to the monastery which was quite nice, but it was the same routine when we went inside to meet 'Mother' as Sister calls her.

At the end of October my Dad had a phone call from Auntie Doris telling him that Grandad was in hospital with chest problems. She said that since the summer he seemed to have lost all interest in life, he did not want to go out at all, stayed in bed or just sat in his chair watching T.V. and not eating properly. Dad asked her to keep him informed and if he got worse he would go up to see him. He told us that Grandad had never been in hospital and could only remember him being off work one week when he had a large carbuncle on his right elbow. He said, "Dad won't like being in hospital with people fussing around him all the time."

So it came as a big shock when Doris phoned five days later telling us that Grandad had died in his sleep on Sunday night. The doctors told her that his heart had just stopped and he had died of old age, he was eighty-three and had had a good life. Dad asked me if I wanted to go to his funeral but I said, "No, I just wanted to remember him as the jolly Grandad who made me laugh".

So Mum said she would stay with me and Dad went up on his own to help Doris with all the arrangements. Dad said it felt strange not seeing Grandad when he arrived in Bingley. Auntie Doris asked Dad to stay with her and they organised everything for the funeral.

When he came back he told me that all the aunties were asking after me, but understood me not wanting to go to Grandad's funeral. He had brought a box of old photographs and papers with him, one was a document to say that when Grandad was ten years old he could start working half days in the mill, where he worked until he retired at sixty five. There were photographs of him as a child and wedding photos of him and his sisters, it must have been a very hard life in those days.

A couple of weeks later, we had a phone call from Bob who was taking me for my Alexandra treatment. He had been on a seminar in London and one of the speakers, Peter Blythe, a psychologist, gave a lecture on the work he was doing with children who have co-ordination difficulties. Bob was very impressed by the lecture and had a long talk with Peter and told him about me and my jerky movements. He asked if the treatment could help me? Peter told Bob that if he brought me to his clinic in Chester he would do an assessment on me.

We all thought it was worth travelling up to Chester to meet Peter Blythe so Bob arranged an appointment for Monday 3rd December. Bob said he would meet us at the clinic at 10.00 a.m. Dad thought it would be a good idea if we went up on the Sunday, then I could have a good nights rest before my assessment. He booked us into a Travel Lodge just outside Chester for Sunday night. We were up early Monday morning, Dad wanted to find the clinic before the roads got busy. It was only a ten minute walk from the centre of Chester, so he parked the car and we had a walk around the city centre and a coffee then went back to meet Bob for our appointment at 10.30 a.m.

Peter Blythe welcomed us into his office, he was a big man with grey hair and a strong voice but a nice friendly smile.

First he told us about his work, telling us that since 1964, when he first set up his own private clinic, he had treated hundreds of children with various problems like behaviour, co-ordination, disturbed aggression, mostly these were referred from various education authorities. During these years he had been made aware that many of the problems children have can be traced back to the foetus in the womb and the first few months of childhood. He explained that, as the baby develops before birth, certain processes take place and also in the early months after birth. If for some unknown reason a baby has not gone through these stages, that's when problems occur.

He then asked my parents many questions, mostly to Mum, about the pregnancy and my birth. She told him about my difficult birth, being in labour for twenty-four hours then having to have a Caesarean section. All the time Peter was watching me, he seemed to know all about it before they had time to answer. He was kind and understanding, knowing how embarrassed I felt with my jerky movements and speech difficulties.

"Well Ann," he said, "I have not worked with many people with your disability and your age but I can certainly improve the quality of your life for you."

Then he told my Dad, "if you are prepared to go ahead with my programme it will entail a lot of hard work for you all. It is expensive and you will get fed up of travelling up to Chester every six weeks for assessment and to update your programme."

He advised us to go have some lunch and come back at 2.00 p.m., then if we wanted to go ahead they would do a full diagnostic assessment and start me on the first stage of the programme.

We walked into the city centre and found a restaurant for lunch. I think we were all a little bewildered, Mum asked Bob what he thought about the treatment. He said, "from the short time I have known Ann I have seen some improvement. If Peter can help her some more I am sure it will be worthwhile."

Dad agreed saying they had always done their best for me, and this maybe my last chance and we should go ahead. Luckily it was a nice day so we walked around the shops and cathedral, then we made our way back to the clinic for two o'clock.

When we went in Peter had a lady with him, he introduced her saying, "this is Joan Young who has been with me for many years. If you want to go ahead we will do the assessment together, then Joan will carry on seeing you on each visit, and I will see you twice a year."

Dad told Peter that we were willing to try his treatment and were prepared to work on it with me. They then asked me to perform certain tasks, making notes of what I could and could not do, then they did some exercises with me laying on my side and turning over, pulling my knees up to my chin. Then sitting in a swivel chair turning first one way and then the other. Peter explained that he had to take me right back to when I was in the womb and work on the movements I should have done before birth. There are key stages when a number of reflexes are released, if some do not happen for any reason they can cause problems later so we had to go through the whole learning process again.

Joan then wrote out my first home programme and explained to Mum how to do the three exercises which I do twice a day, morning and evening. Just before we left, Peter said to me, "Ann you know the reason you move your head from side to side is because your eyes don't move, so you have to turn your head, but don't worry we will work on that as well for you."

"We have taken Ann to hospitals from Leeds to Great Ormond Street in London since she was a baby and no one has ever told us that before," Dad said. He then made an appointment to fit in with his half term at college in February and thanked Joan and Peter and we left for home.

Mum said to me, "It is your birthday in two days time love, but I think what we have heard today is the best present you could ever have received. We will have to have a change of routine now for us all, I am so glad Dad will soon be on holiday for three weeks to help organise everything."

This was another big step in my life. I found the exercise programme very tiring indeed, it took about forty-five minutes to complete the exercises that Joan had given me to do. Two were on the floor and one in my swivel chair which I used when I worked on my typewriter, after I had finished I just had to lay down and rest. Mum also found it hard work with me, she mentioned this to Maureen the district nurse who often called to see us. She told Mum to get in touch with Mrs Shaw who organised home help, meals on wheels and various other things in Alresford. Mum did so and Mrs Shaw said to leave it with her and she would find someone to come in and help us. A few days later two ladies called to see Mum. She was doing my exercise programme so they came in and watched us. When Mum had finished they introduced themselves, one was called Claire, a tall, slim person with long blonde hair, she said that she lived in the next village and had two young children who went to school in Alresford. The other lady was called Joan, she was a small, heavy-built dark-haired lady, older then Claire and lived in Petersfield but worked around the Winchester area.

Mum made us all a coffee and we talked about what help they could be. Mum explained that it was just to help me with all the exercises which take about forty-five minutes to do. Claire said that she was prepared to come in two mornings straight after dropping her children off at school. Joan said she could also manage two mornings but that it would be later around eleven o'clock. Mum was delighted, and it was arranged for Claire to come on Wednesday and Thursday and Joan would come Monday and Friday. Mum told them that they would soon get used to the exercises and thanked them for coming to see us.

After they had left we sat and talked about my routine and the changes we would have to make. Mum said she would contact the Hexagon Centre and the Pinders Centre and explain that I wouldn't be going anymore. Then she told me that, if we only did a short session on a Tuesday, I could still go to Park Place, because she knew that I enjoyed my day there and Dad would help us in the evenings and at weekends.

This was the start of what turned out to be a long four years of hard work for everyone involved. Pete Blythe had given Dad a booklet explaining the work they did at the clinic, there were detailed reports and updates on the progress of some of the patients. Both Claire and Joan read the book and it helped them to understand what we were trying to do and the reasons for the different exercises.

At first we all felt a little as if nothing was happening, then one morning while Claire sat on the floor moving my legs I just rolled over on my own. We were both amazed so Claire put me on my back and told me to try and turn over on my own. After one or two attempts I managed to turn myself over on my tummy, Claire let out a big scream and shouted, "you can do it, Ann". Mum came running to see what the noise was all about.

"I am sorry," Claire said, "I just got so excited for Ann, she has just turned over on her own."

We had to keep a record of any changes in my movements and how I managed with my programme. Dad had phoned Joan Young earlier about the swivel chair one, telling her that five times seemed to stress me, so it was reduced to three times each way.

It was soon half term and time for my next appointment, again we travelled up on the Sunday and stayed at the Travel Lodge overnight. I was eager to see Joan Young again and hear what she had to say about any progress I had made. She went through all my programme with me making notes as we did each exercise and at the end Joan said, "I have found some movement that was not there before which is a good sign, but I am going to leave the programme as it is for another few weeks."

I must have looked disappointed because Joan said, "don't worry Ann, it will take time and we have a long way to go, but I promise you it will work. I will see you again at Easter, just keep on with the same exercises as before."

On our way home both Mum and Dad said, "Try not to be so disappointed Ann, you have made some progress and, like Joan said, it will take time, you are a lot older than the children they usually work with."

So we just carried on with my same programme of exercises. Claire worked very hard with me, we had become good friends and she was very interested in the work Peter and Joan were doing. While we were having coffee after one session Claire told Mum that on Monday afternoons she goes shopping in Alton for some of the old ladies she cares for and wondered if I would like to go with her? Mum said if she was sure she could manage me and all the shopping it would be a nice break for me.

We had great fun on our shopping trips, it was good for me to buy my own things instead of asking mum to get them for me. Claire parked her car in Sainsbury's car park and we did the supermarket shopping first. It was good fun, Claire would pick something off the shelves and say, "do you like these Ann?" then put them in the trolley. She was very organised with all the different shopping lists and knew the layout well so it only took about half an hour to get everything. Claire told me she got all the goods on one bill and then sorted it out at home before taking it to her ladies.

After we left Sainsbury's we walked across into the main street in Alton calling at Woolworths and Boots and last of all 'The Baker's Oven' where we both enjoyed a coffee and a lovely cream cake before going home. Mum thanked Claire for taking me with her, she liked me to be out doing things like everyone else and had always tried to treat me as a normal person.

As the weeks went by I could feel small changes taking place in my body, nothing dramatic but I felt that I could relax for the first time in my life, it was a wonderful feeling.

Chapter Fourteen

At one of our Faith and Light meetings Nancy was telling us that this year the Across Bus was going to Austria. Nancy arranged the annual trips from St. Peter's Church usually they went to Lourdes. This year a new Jumbulance was in service called the Alligator or Bendy Bus, it is like two buses joined together and can bend in the middle. The Across Trust runs these special buses which are fitted out with beds and reclining seats, they have fitted kitchens and medical aids and are used to take sick and disabled people on holidays.

Nancy told us if anyone would like to go they should let her know by the following week as the bus would soon get booked up. As soon as I got home I asked Mum and Dad if I could go to Austria. Mum said, "of course you must go Ann, it is a wonderful opportunity for you to see Vienna, city of dreams where all the beautiful music comes from and a place that I often wanted to visit, I will phone Nancy and ask her to put your name down for the holiday."

The following Tuesday while I was at Park Place and helping Meg in the bookshop an elderly man came in. Meg introduced him saying, "Ann, this is Father Maurice who is staying at Park Place for a few weeks while he recovers from an operation." He came across to talk to me and told me that he was at Basingstoke with Father Havey, but after his operation the doctor said he must rest a few weeks before returning to his parish work.

Over the next few weeks I got to know Father Maurice quite well, after I had finished in the bookshop I usually spent half and hour in the chapel in quiet prayer. Often Father would be there on his own and we would sit and talk. I told him that I knew Father Havey when he was at Chandlers Ford, and I had been to Lourdes with him. He organised the annual pilgrimage for the Portsmouth diocese. I said I enjoyed my day at Park Place as it gave me something to look forward to and I also liked spending time in the chapel. I explained how I wanted to be a nun and had visited one or two orders but because of my handicap they would not take me.

Father was a quiet, gentle man and I found that I could talk to him about anything, he was so understanding. He would say to me, "Ann my dear, you must never give up. Who knows what Our Lord has in store for us all."

I've kept in touch with him and now we are miles apart he phones me every week and has helped me a great deal.

The week before my holiday Nancy held a meeting for everyone going, there was quite a crowd, some people I recognised from church but many I did not know. She introduced a tall, slim man of about forty and said, "this is Raymond, your leader, he will be in charge of everything on your holiday." Raymond was a jolly man and made us laugh by telling us, "You will enjoy your holiday or you'll have me to answer to!" He then explained about the journey. "We'll leave Winchester at 6.45 a.m. on Friday morning," he said, "anyone who's late will be on washing up duty all day! I have ordered Lancashire hotpot for our first meal, after that I don't know. Father Michael will be our chaplain and we will be staying at St. Mary's College, most of you will have heard of the 'The Vienna Boy's Choir' who attend there. I am sure we will all have a good week and enjoy the beauty of Austria."

Nancy then introduced two lovely girls, Rachel and Maria, who would be my helpers for the week we sat and talked until Dad came for me.

The following week seemed to drag by, I could not wait for Friday to come. Mum had been busy getting all my clothes ready and Dad helped her pack and put labels on my case and wheelchair. Mum woke me at 5.30 a.m. with a cup of tea, then helped me to get ready. I did not want any breakfast but she said that I should try and eat something, as I didn't know what time lunch would be. Dad put my things in the car, then Mum gave me a big hug and a kiss and told me to enjoy myself, then we left for Winchester.

As we turned into the car park at St. Peter's I was surprised at the size of the Jumbulance waiting there, it was huge. Raymond was stood there with a clipboard to mark off people as they arrived, then Rachel came across to help me while Dad took my wheel chair and case to the two drivers who were loading the bus. He asked if he could look around the bus and one of the drivers took him on a tour and explained the various pieces of equipment and how it worked, he said that they always had two drivers on the buses so they could travel overnight.

Nancy then started to get everyone on the bus and we were soon ready to move off. Dad gave me a big hug, Rachel told him that they would look after me and then he left for work and we started our journey to Dover. We arrived about midday and boarded the ferry. Raymond told us to take the opportunity and go on deck to stretch our legs as it would be the last time before we arrived in Austria.

Maria and Rachel helped me up onto the deck, there was a nice breeze blowing and as we looked over the White Cliffs of Dover the sun came out. What a lovely sight as the ferry slowly moved out of the harbour, ships of all kinds, and people waving from the shore and the cliffs getting smaller and smaller. Then we went down to the bar for a drink, most of our group were there enjoying the break. After a while there was an announcement over the speakers requesting passengers to return to their cars and buses as we would soon be arriving in Ostend. We all made our way to the bus and settled down, then Raymond told us he was very sorry but he had forgotten to put the oven on, so the meal would not be ready for another hour or so. We all shouted, "we want our hotpot" but it was worth waiting for when it was ready and Rachel fed me as it was a bit awkward on a moving bus.

We travelled from Ostend through Belgium to Brussels and then Germany, there was some lovely scenery all around, everywhere we looked was so clean and bright. We had a hot drink and then got settled for the night, some people were lucky and had beds the others had reclining seats. I could not sleep sitting up, in the end Jonathan put some blankets on the floor for me to see if I could sleep that way, I managed about four hours. As it became daylight Jonathan told me we were still in Germany but would soon be in Austria and should arrive in Vienna at lunch-time.

I just had a bread roll and coffee for breakfast, Raymond was cooking bacon and eggs for anyone who wanted them, he said, "this will be your last English breakfast, make the most of it while you can". Soon the sun came out as we travelled into Austria, this is a very beautiful country with lovely views and buildings.

At long last we arrived in Vienna and everybody cheered, I think people were ready for getting off the bus after the long journey. Raymond told us lunch would be served in the dining room first then our rooms would be allocated to us, and then the rest of the day was free. Father Michael would say Mass at 7.00 p.m. in the college chapel for anyone to attend. As we entered the college I could hear singing. One of the staff told us the boy's choir were practising for a concert later in the week, which we would be able to attend.

After lunch Raymond gave us our room numbers, Rachel, Maria and I shared a large room on the first floor. From the window you could look out over the well-kept grounds which were a mass of colour. After we all had a shower and change of clothes we went for a walk around the gardens and sat for a while and relaxed in the warm afternoon sun.

During the evening meal Raymond gave some announcements out about what we would be doing during the week. He said although we had a full itinerary, we were free to come and go as we pleased, and could just join in the excursions when we wanted. After the meal some of the group suggested going out for a walk and maybe a drink, so we joined them. Not far from the college we found a bar with tables outside so we sat and had a drink. This was our first opportunity for us to get to know each other. Jonathan and another young man called David, came to sit at our table and we all got on well and spent the whole week together. It had been a long day and Rachel said we should try and have an early night so we made our way back to the college and straight to bed. It was lovely to fall into a bed again and I think we were all asleep within minutes of turning out the lights.

It seemed no time at all before Raymond came round knocking everyone up singing *'Oh What A Beautiful Morning'* Maria told him to shut up! It was only 8.00 a.m. There was a small kitchenette where we could make snacks and a drink and we had to make our own breakfast, the college staff only did lunch and evening meals for us. Maria and Rachel spoilt me all week giving me my breakfast in bed then helping me to get ready.

We had lots of fun in the bedroom especially when giving me my shower, there was water everywhere, and we just made it to Mass at 9.30 a.m. in the chapel which most of the group attended.

After Mass Raymond told us lunch would be at midday, then a coach would be available to take us out into the countryside to visit a famous palace. We drove through some picturesque scenery on our way to the palace, which was high up in the hills, there were two guards in bright uniforms at the gold painted gates which they opened for us. Then we followed a winding pathway up to the palace. When it came into view the first thing we saw was the huge golden dome with the sun shining on it, it looked wonderful.

We spent two hours looking round, the rooms were so large and beautifully decorated with paintings and furnishings I have never seen before. I could hear music and as we entered the magnificent ballroom with dozens of bright chandeliers, the orchestra played Strauss' *'Tales from Vienna Woods'*. I could have stayed and listened to the music all day, I have always loved the music of Johann Strauss, Mum used to play me tapes when I was young to try and help me relax and I still do now. We had afternoon tea while we listened to the music then returned to the college by another route for our evening meal.

Jonathan asked us if we were going out but Rachel said we are having a quiet night, so he said that he would go and buy a bottle of wine to share. We sat and talked all evening and it was midnight before we got to sleep.

Raymond came round next morning and told us we are going to spend the full day in Vienna, we could do what we liked and have lunch out, the bus would be there to run us about as we wanted. Jonathan and Dave asked if they could join us, Maria said, "yes, if you push Ann in her wheelchair", so we went off together.

Vienna is the most beautiful city I have every known with magnificent old buildings everywhere and so full of history. It is clean and fresh looking, there are pavement cafes and bars and you can hear music all around you.

We visited St. Stephen's Cathedral, a wonderful building and we were lucky to have a look inside the Opera House. This was breathtaking, I got so excited, I have seen it many time on television when they show concerts from there, especially the 'New Year's Day Concert' which all the family watch together, but to see inside with all the gold and deep red furnishings and thousands of lights, I could just imagine myself in the audience listening to Strauss or Mozart. Jonathan had to drag me out I did not want to leave.

We had lunch, which Dave paid for, and then told us it was very expensive! Then we sat in the square just talking and watching people pass by, we could relax, it seemed like another world so peaceful and everyone so friendly. After looking around a few shops we made our way to the college to change for the evening meal. Later Father Michael, who had brought his banjo with him, played and we all had a good sing-song. Raymond told us to dress up warm the next day as we were going up into the mountains.

We were awakened by Raymond singing, 'The Hills are Alive' at 7.00 a.m. and had no choice but to get up as the coach was leaving at 8.30 a.m. Maria told me to put on a sweater and a pair of trousers as it would be cooler in the mountains.

It was a long journey but the scenery was wonderful especially as we got higher, we passed through soft green meadows with cattle grazing by the clear water of the lakes, then the forest, into the hills and rugged mountains some still had snow on the tops.

Jonathan asked us if we were going on the cable car which we could see in the distance, I was a bit nervous but he said if we all ride together he would look after me. I had seen the cable car swinging high, going from one mountain to another and did not know what to expect as it began to move off. Although it was a breathtaking experience and the views were terrific, I was glad when it was over and I don't think I would do it again.

We had lunch at a restaurant where we sat on the terrace in the warm sunshine, the air was so exhilarating, it was like another world, so quiet and peaceful, we then returned by a different route back to college.

That evening after our meal we were all invited to the concert in the great hall, there was a full orchestra playing and the Vienna Boy's choir sang, most were in Austrian but they did sing some in English for us. It was a lovely end to another exhausting day and one I will always remember.

Next morning at breakfast Raymond told us we were booked on a pleasure boat for a short cruise down the River Danube leaving at 10.00a.m. I was really looking forward to the boat trip, but I must say now I was a bit disappointed, 'The Blue Danube' is not blue anymore, it is a dirty grey, otherwise it was most enjoyable.

It was nice to relax watching the different views as we passed by, there were some beautiful old buildings which looked so elegant, then we travelled through the countryside. A small orchestra played for us and we could request tunes which they would play. We had a nice lunch then made the return journey. As we got near home they played *The Blue Danube Waltz* and everyone sang, it was wonderful.

In the evening Raymond said, "tonight, I am taking you to the best fair you will have seen"; it certainly was. There were all kinds of rides and side shows, but the best was the big wheel. Father Michael told me it was the largest in the world then asked me if I would like to go on with him, of course I said yes. The view from the top was magnificent Vienna lit up at night looked lovely, although it was a bit scary, I did enjoy myself. On our way back Raymond said, "tomorrow we are having a fun day out at a park where there is a large lake, put your old clothes on and we are taking a packed lunch with us."

We had a pleasant journey out into the countryside past small farms with streams running by and there seemed to be wild flowers everywhere. We young ones sat at the back of the bus singing songs from the '*Sound of Music*' we were in a real party mood. Dave shouted, "Oh look there are boats on the lake, let's see if we can all get into one boat and I will row you". It was another glorious day, everyone enjoyed themselves immensely, we sat on the grass and ate our packed lunch, then played games and walked by the lakeside. Maria and Rachel kicked off their shoes then sat with their feet in the water to cool off, I wanted to do the same. Dave and Jonathan were both fooling about and somehow we all ended up in the lake, luckily it was not deep where we were. We soon dried off in the sun before we set off for home. "Tonight," Raymond said on the way back, "we will all have to dress up smart, we are going to a Gala Concert."

Maria said, "I think we had better have a bath after being in the lake, I have some lovely smelly bubble bath we can use", what fun we had, there was foam up to my neck I don't think I have ever had a bath like that. Then we put on our best clothes and went down for our meal, they had done a roast beef and Yorkshire pudding for us and it was good.

The Gala Concert was excellent, the conductor told us Vienna was the land of waltz' of Johann Strauss and Mozart and explained each piece of music the orchestra played. Jonathan sat next to me, he could see that I was enjoying the music and gave me a big hug, this was the highlight of the holiday for me.

"This is our last day," Raymond said at breakfast. "So we are free to do as we like. Father Michael will say Mass this evening then it's a party for everyone." We went to Vienna for a last look round, bought presents to take back for family and friends and just relaxed. That evening, Father Michael gave a nice Thanksgiving Mass for the wonderful time we all had spent together and seeing the wonders that God created for us to enjoy. Then we went into the lounge area where the men had bought some wine and a few nibbles for us to share and a good time was had by all, a perfect end to a smashing holiday.

Raymond called us and said, "we have to pack and clean our rooms before lunch, then the Jumbulance will arrive to load ready to move off at 2.00 p.m." We soon had our things together, then went for a walk in the grounds before lunch. I felt a bit emotional saying goodbye to the staff they had all been so good to us and so welcoming. I think this had been the best holiday I have had and I hope to return one day.

When we had all got seated on the bus we shouted, "Raymond, don't forget to put the oven on." Maria told me she had made sure I had a bed to sleep in this time, I was pleased about that. Travelling back it was nice to see places we passed through during the night on our way out. The scenery was wonderful, so different to England. I managed to sleep quite well in the moving bus, it did not seem to take us as long on the return journey, but I suppose that was just my imagination. Raymond did put the oven on and we had hotpot again, (I don't know where we were when we had it,) then it was Ostend and onto the ferry around 4.00 a.m. in the morning. Raymond told us to have our breakfast on the ferry, luckily the sea was calm for the crossing, then we went on deck to watch the sun rise, what a glorious sight that was. Soon we could see the White Cliffs of Dover and England again.

Mum and Dad were waiting as we arrived back in Winchester, they thanked Rachel and Maria for looking after me and I introduced Dave and Jonathan, they both told Mum it was their pleasure to be in my company. I felt very proud of myself, it had been a wonderful experience for me, one I would not have missed for the world. I said my goodbyes to everyone, although I felt tired I was very happy and had lots of happy memories to look back on.

On our way home Mum and Dad were both very quiet. I had a feeling something was wrong or they were upset for some reason. As soon as we arrived home Mum made us all a drink then asked me to sit down with them. Then she said that Dad had had a phone call from Auntie Florence in Bingley that morning with some bad news. Auntie Doris was very seriously ill in Airedale Hospital, Dad was going up the next day to see her and stay as long as he was needed. He would keep us informed of her condition, and all we could do now was say extra prayers for her swift recovery.

I was very upset because I loved Doris so much, although we did not see her as often now that we lived in Hampshire. Both my Aunties Phyllis and Doris, my Dad's older sisters, were very special to me and had played a large part in my childhood. Over the next few days I recalled the many happy times we had spent together. I always thought of Phyllis and Doris as film stars, they were so beautiful, they had not married and still lived in the family home. I once asked them why and Phyllis just said, "well, no-one ever asked us." Both had lovely voices and sang in the chapel choir and belonged to Bingley Amateur Operatic Society. Many people said Doris should have been a professional, but she was happy as she was. Their house always seemed to be filled with music, I think that is where I learned to appreciate good music.

From being about eighteen months old, Mum used to let me stay for the weekend with them. I really enjoyed that and, of course, they spoilt me. Phyllis, the elder sister, often bought me things, a new dress to wear or toys to play with. Doris was a bit more strict, (but not much). The chapel had played a large part in their lives, as well as being in the choir, they were both Sunday school teachers and would take me with them, I made many friends there.

In summer they took me out on picnics or to the seaside for the day, Blackpool or Morecambe we had lots of fun together. Sundays we went to chapel and Sunday school in the afternoon then for a walk in the park or over Shipley Glen. In winter we would go to the cinema to see children's films and to the pantomime in Bradford and Leeds. It is funny how little things sticks in your mind. One Saturday we had been to the park in Bradford, Phyllis had bought me a pink handbag to match my dress. We sat on a seat waiting for the bus home and it was not until we were nearly home, that Doris noticed my handbag was missing, she was so upset she got off the bus and went back to find it. Luckily an old gentleman was sat on the seat with the bag, he told Doris he was going to hand it into the park warden, so she got it back for me.

When Phyllis died, Doris asked mum if I could still go to stay at weekends, Mum said of course I could and this seemed to help Doris as she was missing Phyllis very much and we became very close.

I loved my Saturday evenings the best, after Doris had given me my bath and I was in my night clothes we would sit together and have a cuddle on the settee talking about all kinds of things. She once told me, "Ann, I am always here for you if anything should happen to Mum and Dad remember I will look after you." We had a special kind of relationship I just cannot explain it. I remember when I was about ten years old and pestering my parents to let me go to boarding school, Doris was very upset and told me that she would miss me so much.

When I started at St. Rose's in Gloucester, Doris came with us to see me settled in. I always think that she would have liked to have been one of the housemothers looking after the girls. My Dad would bring her down with them to the garden fete in June, and they would stay for the weekend and take me out. She was there with them to see me walk the first time on my own. The Sisters had kept that as a surprise, when dad's car stopped at the main entrance I walked out to meet them. I think both Mum and Doris cried. I would see Doris when I was home on school holidays and stay with her often. In 1978 when Mum and Dad moved down to Hampshire for work reasons, Doris was very sad, she missed us all very much, but would come down to stay with us at holiday time, or we went to her house.

My Dad left for Yorkshire early Sunday morning to visit Doris in hospital, he phoned Mum and the news was not good. She was crying when she came off the phone and said that Doris was on a life support machine and very, very poorly. Dad stayed in Bingley a week, sitting with Doris all day, he would phone us twice a day but there was no change in Doris' condition and the doctors advised Dad to come home for a break, saying they would contact him if there was any change. When Dad arrived home he looked terrible, I have never seen him like that before.

That night we all sat down together and he told us the whole story. "Ann, this will upset you but I am afraid you have to know what happened. Doris came home from work, and after tea she answered a knock at the door and a man with a knife pushed her inside. She ran to the front door screaming loudly but he caught her in the hallway. They think he must have panicked because he stabbed Doris twelve times, she was rushed to hospital still conscious and told them what had happened. After massive surgery and drugs she is on a life support machine but it is touch and go whether she will pull through."

I began to cry, Mum gave me a cuddle, I think we were all in tears, Dad told us to pray for Doris and hope she would recover. I went into my bedroom and just broke my heart, I loved Doris so much I could not stop crying.

My dad rang the hospital, morning and evening, but there was no change in her condition, then early one morning about six a.m. the hospital phoned, it was one of the doctors wanting my dad to go up there straightaway, which he did. Later in the day he phoned Mum, when she came off the phone she burst into tears then held me tight. As we sat together she told me poor Doris was not responding to the treatment and had suffered a relapse.

"The doctors have told Dad that she cannot survive without the life support machine, and have asked for permission to turn the unit off and to let Doris die." Mum said. That was why Dad rang, to ask Mum what he should do. Mum told him to do what was best for Doris, she must not suffer anymore. She said, "Ann, I am sorry but we have to face up to this and be strong. At least she will be with Phyllis and their mum and dad at peace together."

My dad stayed in Bingley a week, the police needed to see him because it was now a murder inquiry, the first in Bingley for fifty years. There would be extra men called in to help them catch the man who had stabbed Doris.

They had to go with him to the house as it was still a crime scene with a police constable on duty outside. He told us later about the hallway with blood everywhere. Then said Auntie Florence was very good and had helped him to clean up as best they could. Auntie was so upset as Doris had spent quite a lot of time with her since we had moved down south, she said that it should never have happened to her, Doris was a good, kind person always helping others and she was only in her fifties.

The coroner wanted to see Dad and explained that there would have to be a post-mortem and inquest, but he could not tell him when we would be able to have the funeral. In fact we had to wait about six weeks before they let us bury Doris, it was a very trying time for us all. One good thing, the police told Dad just before he came home that they had arrested a man and that he would be charged with Doris' murder.

I could see that Dad was very upset when he arrived home, he told us that the doctors did all they could for Doris, but her wounds were so severe. He said maybe it was for the best, Doris would never have been the same person after such an horrific attack, and she would have been too frightened to live on her own again. Then he told mum we would have to go up at half-term to clear the house out and see about selling it. I realised then that I only had Mum and Dad now as family, apart from some very old aunties still living in Bingley.

The police informed us later that the man they had arrested had been in court. He admitted stabbing Doris and was being held in Armley prison until the trial which would be at the Leeds Assizes.

We had lots of phone calls and letters from friends and people who had known Doris, especially the members of the chapel where the family had worshipped for many years. It was a comfort to know how well liked Doris was and how well our whole family were thought of, so many people would miss her.

Half-term came and we went up to Bingley and stayed with some friends. I did not want to go to the house ever again, so Auntie Florence went to help them with the massive task of clearing the house. Mum told me later that they found all Phyllis's things still there and she had been dead sixteen years. It was very emotional for dad having to go through all the documents of both Phyllis and Doris. They managed to clear everything during the week and put the house up for sale. Dad brought a lot of the paper work home with him to sort through, he said that he felt very sad seeing the house empty and the 'for sale' sign outside, it was the end of an era for him.

About two weeks later we had a letter from the coroner saying that, provided that Doris was buried, we could go ahead with the funeral, we were very pleased that now at last we could lay Doris to rest.

My Dad contacted Jack Bailey, a family friend, and also funeral director who would make all the arrangements for us so that the funeral could take place as soon as possible. This would be a difficult time for everyone. As we travelled up to Bingley once again I asked Mum if I had to attend because I knew that I would break down if I went. Mum said, "Ann, you do not have to go if it is going to upset you, I do not want to go myself but Dad will need me with him to support him through this ordeal."

Mum phoned Sister Pascal at the convent in Keighley, a very dear friend of ours, to ask if I could stay with them for the day. Sister said they would be only too pleased to have me, and told Mum that Doris had been in their prayers from the first day of this tragedy. Dad had to see the minister who was taking the service, he had known Doris many years, and was very sad at the way she had

135

died. He told Dad that extra seating had been brought in because so many people wanted to attend to say farewell to a special person.

Mum and Dad took me on to the convent about ten a.m. They made us very welcome, telling us that it had been a great shock when they heard about Doris. Sister Pascal then invited us for a meal in the evening so we could relax a little after the day's ordeal.

Unknown to me Sister had phoned Eileen Varley, she was my godmother, and asked her to come to the convent for lunch with us. It was such a lovely surprise, I had not seen Eileen since we left Keighley twelve years before. We had lots to catch up on, she was surprised to see how much I had grown and told me that I was a proper young lady now. I told her all about my time at St. Rose's and the further education college at Newhaven, and my life now back at home.

At 2.30, the time of the funeral, we joined all the Sisters in the convent chapel to say prayers for Doris. Unfortunately Eileen could not stay to see Mum, I said she would be sorry to have missed her, but I would give her the news.

Mum and Dad came about half past five looking very sad and weary, it had been a really hard day for them. Dad told us everything had gone well, the chapel was crowded and people were standing outside, both T.V. and Press reporters were there. Then they said the minister gave a lovely talk about Doris, and all that she had done for the chapel and Sunday school, especially her singing and the life she had lived, and how sad that it was cut short so brutally.

Mum then looked at me and said, "I am so glad that you were here with the Sisters Ann, it was so emotional, I think everyone had tears in their eyes, I know I had. There was a police escort from the chapel to the cemetery, which only the family attended. All the main roads were crowded with people as we passed by. I never expected anything like that, the murder had been the main news item in the Press and on local television for weeks."

I think we all felt a sense of relief, now at last we had been able to lay Doris to rest. She would always be there in my heart, a dear, dear auntie who I would never ever forget. We stayed and had a lovely meal with the Sisters, they had known Doris and it helped me a lot just being with them and talking about the many happy times that we had spent together.

Next day Dad had to see the police again, and the solicitors before we set off back home. It was good to get back into the old routine again, doing my exercises with Claire and Joan. We had an appointment in Chester in two weeks time, I had been on this programme a year, and I was eager to see Peter Blythe again to see what progress I had made.

Mum suggested that we have a short break in Chester, and do our Christmas shopping as well as the visit to the clinic. She said we won't be going to Bingley this time and it will be a nice change for us.

Chester looked lovely with decorated trees and fairy lights everywhere, and the shop window displays were wonderful. I like the olde world look of the shops, they are so quaint and so full of history, I would have loved to have lived in those days. We enjoyed doing our Christmas shopping, and also went to the carol service in the cathedral, which was really excellent.

Peter Blythe welcomed us then sat in while Joan went through my programme with me, he said, "I can see that you have been working very hard Ann, with a lot of improvement you are not as tense now." He then asked Joan to try two more different exercises with me, telling Mum these should help me to be more in control of my movements, but, he said, if I found it too tiring, I should do half the programme in the morning and the rest at night. We thanked them both, saying it was hard work but now we could see some improvement, we knew it was well worthwhile. Then we went and had a good Christmas lunch before going home.

I do not think any of us really enjoyed Christmas that year I know my thoughts were about Doris, and the terrible way that she had died. In my own mind I had been looking ahead to when she would be retired, because she had told me that she may move nearer to us, so that we could spend more time together, but that would never happen now.

In January Dad had a letter from the solicitors in Bingley telling him that the house had now been sold and they could finally wind up Doris's affairs. There was only the trial now, which would take place at the end of June.

Chapter Fifteen

I did not realise just how much the death of my dear Auntie Doris would mean to me, and it made me take a new look at my own life in a different way. Living with my parents I felt secure with nothing to worry me, they cared for me and, with help, I could do anything I wanted.

Now they were my only family and it made me think what would happen to me if they were both killed in a car accident or something. I had never really looked ahead or thought about my life like this before, it was very frightening for me, but I did not want to tell Mum and Dad, it was something that I had to do myself.

At the Hexagon Centre there were a few clients that I knew who lived in care homes, so I talked to them and asked them about life in a home, they all told me the best way was to go on respite care in a home and see for myself. Maxine had recently moved into a new home in Boyat Wood, she told me there were six self contained flats and two blocks of four rooms for respite care. Maxine was in a flat and looked after herself with help when she needed it. The respite unit was fully staffed with a manager over the whole complex.

I knew that I would have to contact my social worker and of course Social Services would be involved with funding. This was all new to me but, I was an adult in my own right and it was my responsibility. This was the time that I had to talk to my parents about what I wanted and my reasons for wanting to try living away from home. I love Mum and Dad very much and did not want to hurt them in any way whatsoever, so I had to try and explain how I was feeling.

Mum was very upset about it all and told me to put such thoughts out of my mind. Dad said he understood how I felt but said it was too soon for me to leave home. Around that time I must admit I had a very stubborn streak in me and I told my parents that my mind was made up and I would contact my social worker and look for a home.

I soon realised it was not going to be as easy as I thought. There are very few homes for young, adult, physically disabled people anywhere around the country, which surprised me very much. My social worker said he would put me on the waiting list for respite care at Boyat Wood, which was run by Winchester Social Services.

About two months later I received a letter saying a place was available for me in May and I should contact the manager to arrange a visit and confirm my dates. The manager was a very nice man and showed me around the unit, he explained how the respite care worked telling me that they encouraged each client to do as much for themselves as they could but care staff were on duty 24 hours a day.

It was agreed that I should go the last two weeks in May. Mum and Dad took me down and helped me settle in my room, which was quite large. There was a wardrobe, set of drawers and a bedside table, I took my radio cassette player and TV with me. Each unit had four bedrooms and a dining/lounge area plus their own kitchen where you could make a drink and snacks.

I soon made friends with the other clients in my unit, and the care staff who were there to help us. It did not take me long to realise that I was not as able as I thought, I could not even make myself a drink, so it would not be possible for me to live on my own in a flat. In a way I was glad of the experience the two weeks at Boyat Wood gave me, and I knew now that I would have to look for a care home.

A few weeks later I was with a group in South Sea for the day and recognised one of the boys, David Taylor who used to attend the Hexagon. We got talking and he told me he now lived in a new home just outside Portsmouth, and went to a work centre in Cosham. He said there were only six residents and it was like a big family unit and he was happy there. I asked him for the name and address of the home so that I could contact them.

The following week I wrote to the home and asked if I might visit them to see what it was like. I had a nice letter to say I could visit them on the Saturday afternoon and have a look around and to talk to the residents.

Mum and Dad realised that I was determined to go and live in a home. Although they did not agree with me they took me down to see it. The home was called Wynscome and Mr & Mrs Rutter owned and ran it. The house stood in its own grounds set off the main road. Mr. Rutter had built the home himself, on the ground floor, there were six bedrooms plus bathrooms and toilets a large lounge, dining area and a kitchen, the Rutters lived in the rooms above.

We looked around the home and talked to residents, who were about my own age, all said they were very happy living there. I could tell Mum was not keen on me going there, but she knew how determined I was and just said, "I hope it all works out well for you Ann."

"Don't worry too much about mum," Dad said, "she just cares very much about you and wants you to be happy. Anyway, if it doesn't work out you can always come back home." I had a feeling that is what they both wanted, but they also knew I was determined to stand on my own two feet.

Janet Rutter who ran the home with her husband said that she could move David and Mark in together then I could have a room to myself which was what I wanted. They suggested that I go on a month's trial to see how I settled and I could start in September.

Mum took me shopping into Basingstoke to buy new clothes and things for my room. Dad made me a desk unit where I could put my TV and typewriter. They helped me move in on the Sunday. I was a bit apprehensive about it when the time came, but Dad said we are only 25 miles away and will visit you anytime.

My room was at the front of the house with a patio door and you could see for miles across the countryside. What a lovely view, and in the warm weather I opened the door and sat outside. I soon made friends with all the residents, some went to the Hexagon centre where I went and some went to a new centre, the Horizon in Cosham, about five miles from the home.

I asked Janet if I could carry on going to Park Place on a Tuesday, as this was my favourite day. She told me that would be fine as the mini bus could drop me off on the way to the Hexagon and collect me at tea-time. Things seemed to be working out for me and I was happy there. Dad would collect me on Sunday morning we would go to Mass at Park Place then home for Sunday lunch with mum.

At the end of my month there Janet told me that my social worker would be coming to review my stay and discuss my future.

The meeting went very well and it was agreed that I could stay at Winscome, it was suggested that as the Cosham day centre was nearer, all the residents should attend there.

I went for assessment to the Horizon, which was a new centre. The staff were very friendly, and I also met some clients who used to attend the Hexagon Centre, so I had no worries about moving, though I would miss the many friends that I had made at the Hexagon. I'd had five very happy years there and I felt very sad saying goodbye. I thanked Mr Gale and Mr Wilson and of course Mrs Hancock for all their help, they all said it had been a pleasure to have known me and wished me luck when I started at the Horizon.

My life was very busy now attending the day centre and Park Place and not having my Mum there, I soon realised how much she had done to make life easy for me. Now I had to organise my own life, remembering to put straws in my bag and make sure I was ready for the bus. These are all small things which I took for granted and just assumed they were done. It came as a big shock to me, I had now to think for myself and if things were not done it was my own fault.

One evening while we were having our meal, Janet and Tony sat with us, they asked us if anyone would like to go on holiday to Swanage in Dorset. They had received a brochure from the Malbury Hotel which was suitable for disabled people with care staff to help them. I said straightaway that I would love to go and David and Mark also wanted to go. Janet was not too keen on Mark going as he was very quiet, I said to her, "Don't worry about Mark, I will look after him". I could tell he really wanted to go on holiday.

As the weeks went by we began to get excited, especially Mark, he told me that he had never been on a proper holiday before and asked me if I would look after him. I said of course I would and he said he would be good for me. At long last the big day arrived, there was a knock on my door and Mark came in. I said, "What are you doing Mark? It is only 6.00 a.m." He said, "I have been awake ages, I am just so excited about my holiday." Tony must have heard us and came down and said, "Well if you are all awake we may as well make an early start and beat the traffic jams."

We soon had breakfast and Tony put the bags and wheelchairs in the mini bus and we were away by 7.30 a.m.

The day started well, as we travelled the sun began to come up. We were all very happy we were singing along to a tape that Tony put on in the bus. Around 10.30 we stopped in the New Forest for morning coffee and a break for Tony, we sat outside a café. Tony said, "it looks like we will be in Swanage far too early as you are not supposed to go into the hotel before 2.00 p.m. so we'd better find a nice pub where we can have a bit of lunch." We went though the New Forest, which was lovely. Little Mark enjoyed seeing the horses.

At long last we arrived in a nice place called Wareham, it was a little olde world sort of a town with old fashioned shops. We had lunch in a pub overlooking the river, I think we were all glad of the break.

Mark asked me how far we had to go? I told him not very far and about half an hour later we saw a sign saying 'welcome to Swanage'. Tony drove us along the front, I was really amazed to see the golden coloured sand and it was nice to see children playing on the beach. We went passed the little theatre and saw that they were showing *'The Boy Friend'*. Tony asked us if we would like to go, if we did he would book it for us then ask the staff to make sure we got there.

At long last we arrived at the Malbury Hotel, it looked lovely from the outside. There were three nice ladies to welcome us, Jean, the manager introduced Maureen, the housekeeper to us. She was a jolly person with a northern accent, then there was a pretty young lady called Vicky who Jean said would be my helper. Tony explained to them what help we required then Jean said to him, "do not worry we shall make sure they have a nice fortnight's holiday." Tony thanked them and said to me, "Ann, you are in charge" then he left.

Vicky asked us if we would like to have a cup of tea, then she would show us our rooms, she was a tall slim young lady with long brown hair and told us she lived just down the road and her husband was a policeman.

As we sat having our tea we could hear an organ playing, Mark asked where the music was coming from? Vicky said that it was Jean's husband playing. We looked around the hotel, the dining room was all set up for the evening meal and looked so inviting. There was a large lounge with a stage at one end and a bar, Vicky told us that people came in every night to entertain the guests, except Saturdays, when all the guests get to know each other, "Jim plays the organ and we have a sing-song."

We then went up in the lift to our bedrooms, the room I had was at the back of the house but from the window I could see the harbour and cliffs in the distance. The room was quite big with its own shower and toilet. Vicky helped me unpack as we were talking and getting to know each other. She asked if we were brother and sister and where we lived. I said, "Oh no we just live together with four other people, but Janet who runs the home asked me to look after Mark as he has no family of his own."

I then got changed and went to find the boy's room, a nice young man was looking after them so I just told them to get changed and I would see them in the lounge. At 6.30 p.m. the gong went for our meal, Vicky showed us to our table. She said, "Maureen has given you a nice table in the corner so the staff can keep an eye on you in case you need help". When all the guests were settled Maureen welcomed everyone and hoped that we would enjoy our stay with them, telling us, "I have ordered good weather for you." We all laughed!

The meal was delicious it was soup or melon to start with then roast lamb with all the trimmings and trifle or ice cream, we were all ready for it. A waiter came round to ask if we would like a drink from the bar. Mark asked me if he was allowed? I said, "oh yes, we are on holiday now."

When we had finished the beautiful meal we went into the lounge and sat and talked. Vicky brought over a round of drinks. I could tell Mark and David were enjoying themselves. They said, "we are glad you are with us", I felt happy for them.

During the evening we got to know some of the guests, there was a nice young couple with a lovely little girl called Sara. They came over to talk to us, what a good chat we had. Sara's parents told us that Sara was blind, but she was very cheerful. During the evening

Jean's husband played the organ for us, it was lovely to listen to. After a while Vicky came to sit with us to see what we were thinking of doing tomorrow, I said we hadn't thought about it and she said, "well tomorrow afternoon there is a band on top of the hill where you can look over the sea we can take you and come back for you if you would like, we said we would. About 10.30 p.m. I noticed Mark getting tired so I said we'd all had a long day and I thought it was time for bed. Mark said, "but Ann we are on holiday do I have to?"

"Yes," I said.

As soon as I hit the pillow I was asleep, it didn't seem long before Vicky woke me with a cup of coffee. As she was helping me to have my shower she was saying that this weekend was Swanage Carnival and the hotel was putting a float in this year, the theme was country and western. Vicky asked me if we would like to go on it? I said, "oh yes please I am sure we would." She said she would take me to Mass as the church was just down the road. When I was ready I thanked Vicky for helping me. We went to breakfast, Mark and David were already down. Mark looked so happy, I asked them if they had both slept well, they said they had.

Mark asked, "what are we doing today?"

"Well," I replied, "this morning I am going to Mass, so why don't you men make the most of the sun."

About 8.55 a.m. the gong went for breakfast Mark ask me what we'd have and I said all kinds of cereal then he could have a full English or just some toast. Vicky came over to see if we were OK. After breakfast I told the men to do what they wanted this morning, so David said, "Don't worry about us Ann we will be OK till you come back". Vicky asked me if she could come to see *'The Boy Friend'* with us? I said, "Oh yes please do". Vicky took me to Mass it was a lovely little church.

After a wonderful lunch of roast chicken and all the trimmings we got ready to listen to the band. Vicky pushed me and there were two handsome waiters who pushed the men. The band was beautiful to listen to, the views from the top of the hill were superb, you could see across the bay. We all enjoyed it.

Luckily, it was good weather each day and the staff were so good to us the whole fortnight. Each afternoon they used to take us down to the seafront and come back for us in three hours. We loved sitting on the seafront watching the people enjoying themselves. In the evening we used to sit in the lounge talking to the other guests. On Tuesday I suggested that we had a fairly early night as we would be late on the Wednesday, I don't think Mark was amused but David went with him. I told them to have a bath Wednesday afternoon and put on their best clothes, as we were going to the theatre to see *'The Boy Friend'*.

Wednesday we just had a quiet day. Vicky gave me a smashing bath and said she was looking forward to the show. We had an early evening meal, the men looked really smart and I was proud of them. As it was a pleasant evening Vicky suggested that we would walk down. Two porters pushed Mark and David, Vicky pushing me. The show was excellent full of colour, and wonderful music, we really enjoyed it. We thanked Vicky and the porters for taking us. By the time we got in it was going on for midnight, we got some chips and watched the sea, it was a wonderful sight, a perfect end to a perfect day.

The next day we had a very quiet day, Mark and Dave thanked me for taking them to the theatre, I said it was a pleasure to have them with me. Mark said, "oh dear we have only got four more days."

"Yes but we have the carnival to look forward to."

The next few days were very busy for all the staff at the hotel preparing for the carnival, Vicky said we would go and help them get the lorry ready. Luckily one of the porters said, "They say it's going to be a very hot weekend." What fun we had decorating the lorry with streamers and balloons, it looked lovely. Vicky told me that she had found some cowboy hats and some clothes to wear. Someone got some hay from a nearby farm for the floor of the lorry and we put stools and tables on from the bar. We were all very tired by the end of the day. Vicky suggested that she would give me my bath tomorrow evening after we had been on the float.

Next morning at breakfast David looked tired, I asked him if he was OK and he replied, "I did not sleep very well, Mark was too excited about being in the carnival." At breakfast Jean told all the guests it would be just a buffet lunch so everyone had to help themselves, but, she said she would make sure we had a good evening meal.

After lunch Vicky helped me to change into my cowgirl outfit, she also got changed and we both looked smart, even the men looked great. Around 12.30 p.m. we began to load the lorry, the weather was warm and sunny, everyone was happy and enjoying themselves.

We moved off to join the parade, I was amazed to see so many different types of floats all beautifully decorated each with its own theme. There were marching bands and majorettes and people dressed as clowns and in funny costumes walking in procession, as it went along the seafront where crowds of people were stood waving. Then we went around the town and back the other way along the seafront, what an experience for us all. Young Mark really enjoyed himself we must have been on the float about four hours.

In the evening we had a wonderful meal. Jean told us that our float had won second prize, then said, "the drinks are on me tonight to say thank you for all the hard work you put in". We sat talking in the lounge, then Mark said to me, "I don't want to go home tomorrow, I have had a lovely holiday."

I felt a bit sorry for him but said, "look Mark, you have some lovely memories to look back on, and there is always next year to plan for so don't be sad".

The next morning Vicky said, "If I help you pack now then after breakfast we can go shopping and have a last walk along the seafront". Two porters helped David and Mark, then we set off for the shops. I bought Mum and Dad a present and the men bought Janet and Tony a present, then we walked by the harbour for a last look at the sea, then back to the hotel for lunch.

Tony arrived at 2.00 p.m., paid our bill, thanked everyone for looking after us and loaded the mini bus. I thanked Vicky for all her help and promised to keep in touch. Mark told Jean that he would see her next year and to keep a room for him, then we got into the bus and waved to everybody. It had been a wonderful holiday, Mark looked at me and said, "thank you Ann for looking after me, I have never been so happy".

We had lots to talk about when we got back and loads of photographs to show everyone. Mark was telling them about being in the Carnival parade and riding on a lorry, he was so happy.

Chapter Sixteen

Life for me seemed to be nice and settled now and I was quite happy living at Winscome but I did not know then it would not stay that way. While we were on holiday Tony had been given planning permission to build another six rooms on to the house, this would double the number of residents in the home. Janet did not employ any more staff and it was not long before I realised they were in it for the money not our welfare. Care standards had dropped, the staff were too busy now to help us like they had and there was a bad atmosphere in the home.

Mum soon realised something had happened and asked me if I was happy, when I told her about all the changes she was very upset. Mum and Dad went to see Janet to talk about it, she just said, "if Ann is not happy, take her home, I can soon fill her room."

Mum asked me what I wanted to do I just said, "please mum can I come home with you?" I did wonder if I would ever find the right place to live, I wanted to be as independent as I could and also to let Mum and Dad have a life of their own without having to worry about me.

So I went back home to live in Alresford and tried to get my life together again. I continued going to Park Place every Tuesday, it became my main stay. Sister Evelyn used to talk to me a lot. I called her my second mum she seemed to understand my feelings and kept reassuring me that things would work out.

Not long after I was back home my Dad had a letter from the Crown Court in Leeds, the date had been set for the trial of the murder of Auntie Doris. We were all on edge about this and had been waiting to hear from the court. The only good thing, they said that my Dad would not be called as a witness, it was a big relief for him. He had told me that he did not want to go to the trial, saying it would be too painful for him to sit and listen to all the details coming out.

He phoned a very good friend of ours, Beryl, who lived in Leeds, she had just retired from work and told him that she would attend the trial for us and keep us up-to-date on the proceedings.

The trial at Leeds Assizes went on for three weeks, the 25 year old man, Jeremy Bradbrooke, at first denied he was the killer, then he changed his plea, telling the court that he was the reincarnation of Conan the Barbarian! His counsel said he had a split personality and was not responsible for his actions but the Crown had a top London doctor who had examined Mr Bradbrooke on a number of occasions. He told the court that he had an over exaggeration of fantasies, once he said he had been a professional football player, another time that he had been a soldier in the Falklands War where his best friend was killed. All these stories were checked out but were proved to be lies.

The Crown's case was that Bradbrooke had split from his partner the day before and set out to find sex. He was dressed in T shirt and jeans with a track suit over them, he also carried a knife. He travelled from Bradford where he lived to Bingley, it was a lovely sunny day. He saw Doris Whitaker sat on a deck chair in the front garden on her own. He went round the back and rang the bell, when she answered the door he had the knife in his hand. He then pushed her into the house, she screamed and ran to the front door, but he pulled her away, shut the door and stabbed her many times in the back. She fell to the floor but again tried to get up, then he stabbed her through the chest.

He ran away getting rid of the knife and track suit in a nearby bin, before going home. Meanwhile Doris's next-door neighbour had heard the screams, and ran in to find Doris on the floor bleeding, she phoned for the ambulance and the police and tried to help her. Doris was able to say what had happened before she passed out, she was rushed to hospital and underwent massive surgery, she was in intensive care and did recover for a while but sadly died two weeks later.

The police said at the trial that the day after Doris died they had a phone call from a women saying she was Bradbrooke's partner and he had told her about the incident. She told them, "I did not know how serious it was but when I heard this woman had died I knew that I must report it."

The jury only took 75 minutes to reach their verdict that he was guilty. The judge told Bradbrooke that he had been found guilty of a horrible and senseless murder of a well liked and wholly innocent woman. "You entered her house and threatened her with a knife, when she sought to run away you dragged her back and stabbed her many times. There is only one sentence I can pass on you that is imprisonment for life."

Beryl used to phone Dad every evening with a full report on the case and she sent him cuttings from the local paper. Of course this was big news both for TV and the media, also we had many calls from friends who had been at court. We were all just glad it was over and he was found guilty.

I will just say my Dad has helped me to write this part as I still miss my dear Auntie Doris very much and have found this very hard to do.

A few weeks later Mum had a letter from Park Place, they were having a weekend retreat to prepare for Advent and Sister Evelyn thought we would be interested. Mum said to me, "Ann this is just what you need. Will you come with me, we can do it for Auntie Doris. It will help us to clear our minds of this dreadful thing. I know that you will never forget Doris, she has been a large part of your life but maybe we can lay her to rest now." I told Mum that I would love to go with her, she wrote straight away to put our names down for the retreat.

The weekend Mum and I were away, Dad phoned the hotel they stayed at in Eastbourne to ask if they were open over Christmas time, the manager said they were and they had a 'Christmas Special' four day stay and he would send him a brochure. Mum was not too keen on the idea of going away at Christmas, but between us we persuaded her that she needed a break, it would save her doing all the shopping and cooking, she would be able to relax and be waited on instead.

We had never been to a hotel at Christmas before and we liked Eastbourne so we were all looking forward to it. There were about thirty people booked in, the lounge and dining room were beautifully decorated and a massive Christmas tree stood in the entrance hall. Our rooms were at the front of the hotel and from the windows you could see fairy lights all along the seafront, what a wonderful sight. After the evening meal we just sat in the lounge, a man was playing the organ it was just nice to relax in the friendly atmosphere and chat.

The next day was Christmas Eve, Mum said she would like to look around the shops. Eastbourne has a good shopping centre with some large stores. When I was at F.E. College in Newhaven we often came along the coast to Eastbourne at weekends. The town was busy with people doing their last minute shopping, but it was a change for us to be there. The hotel were just doing bar snacks for lunch, so Dad said we may as well eat out instead of going back to the hotel.

As we walked by the Town Hall the Salvation Army were playing carols, I have always had a soft spot for the army. When I was about eight years old a neighbour, Mrs. Sale, who was in the Army and in charge of the Girl Guides encouraged me to go with her. Dad always said I looked smart in my uniform, they do a lot of very good work and are really friendly people. I was with them until we moved down south.

As we made our way back to the hotel, Dad said, "I think we should walk by the church to see what time Mass is." We had just turned down the road and you could see people going into church, Mum asked a lady what was happening and she said it was their carol service and that everyone was welcome so we went and joined in. During the service, which was lovely, the priest gave out the times of the Masses. Dad asked us which Mass we would like to attend. Mum suggested that, as we were on holiday, we should go to Midnight Mass then have a lie in on Christmas morning, everyone agreed.

The evening meal was wonderful, I have never seen so much food around. This was followed by a Cabaret show, which was first class.

Then just after eleven o'clock we went to our rooms to get ready for Mass, it was a fine clear night so we walked to church. I loved the Christmas Mass, there was a good choir, the church was full and I had a lovely feeling inside me as the priest processed with the altar boys and laid the infant child in the crib. What a moving service it was and the priest gave a short homily telling us that this was the anniversary of the birth of Christ, a time both to look back to the life we have lived and to look ahead and maybe try that bit harder to live a better life, be a better person to be more forgiving and let Christ come into our hearts. I am sure everyone came out of church feeling very humble.

Mum woke me with a cup of tea at nine o'clock saying "Happy Christmas sleepy head", when she opened the curtains I could see lots of blue sky and lovely sunshine. Mum helped me dress then we went down to the dining room, my parents had had their breakfast I just had fruit juice and toast. Dad asked me if I would like to go for a walk and get some fresh air. "Christmas lunch is at one thirty," he said, "and we will probably be inside all day." So we set off along the seafront, there were quite a lot of people walking it was so refreshing.

When we got back to the hotel Mum gave me a parcel, inside there was a beautiful pale blue dress. Then Dad handed me a gift box, when I opened it I could see a lovely pearl necklace, I was so thrilled. Mum helped me dress and put the necklace on when I looked at myself in the mirror Dad told me, "you look a proper young lady now Ann, so grown up." I did not know what to say, I just gave them a big kiss and a hug.

As we entered the dining room we were handed a glass of sherry, they had moved all the tables into a horseshoe shape, everyone together instead of separate tables. The food was so delicious, there must have been five or six different courses each looked and tasted excellent and we had wine to drink.

The atmosphere was warm and friendly, we pulled Christmas crackers and wore paper hats. As the meal came to an end the waitresses came round with a tray of presents for all the guests, the ladies got a small piece of jewellery and the men a pen and pencil set, and of course toys for the children.

We all then moved into the lounge to play party games, nearly everyone joined in and it was great fun. An open buffet had been laid out in the dining room so people could help themselves when they felt like it. In the evening an entertainer came in and of course the bar was open, it was so nice to see people enjoying the festivities, especially Mum and Dad.

Boxing Day was another fine day we had a quiet morning then in the afternoon we went for a run in the car up to Beachy Head and the South Downs. In the distance we saw the Boxing Day hunt ride by, it was so colourful, riders in their red jackets and white jodhpurs and lovely horses with the pack of hounds out in front. It is a nice sight, but I don't think I believe in blood sport there must be other, more humane, ways to kill animals.

That evening a four piece band played for dancing, they had a lovely young lady singer who had a wonderful voice. I asked Mum if she had enjoyed the break, she said, "yes it had been lovely to get away, not to think about cooking meals or anything and being waited on by everyone". I told her she looked better, the change had been good for her.

We were up nice and early next morning, after another good breakfast we packed our things, said our goodbyes and were on our way home by eleven o'clock. Mum wanted some shopping, so we stopped in Chichester, went round the shops, had a meal then straight home.

It was nice to be back home in Alresford for New Year. The Rotary Club had organised a United Service in St. John's Church on New Year's Eve, then fireworks in the square. The church was full and it was a lovely service, as the church clock struck twelve the bell ringers began to ring in the New Year and we all wished each other a Happy New Year. We were stood watching the fireworks when it began to snow, gentle flakes falling from the sky. Alresford is a very old picturesque little town, it looked so pretty in the moonlight with a covering of snow on the roof tops as we made our way home.

I was surprised when I woke next morning to see deep snow everywhere, we had not seen much snow since we moved down south. It was like in my childhood back in Yorkshire, how I used to love playing in the snow, Dad would build me a big snowman in the garden and I'd try to make snowballs, with not much success. Then he'd sit me on a sledge, pull me up the hills and I'd sit between his legs and fly down to the bottom, what fun we had. Mum used to get upset when we came home wet through, but she liked us to have fun. The local people could not cope with the snow, they were frightened of driving their cars on the roads which did not get cleared. Dad said, "let's make the most of it Ann, it won't stay long". Everyone thought we were mad playing out in the snow, I was glad Dad was still on holiday, he was right, after a couple of days the snow began to melt away.

At the college where Dad worked they always had conference day before they began a new term, he says it is just so the Chairman and the Bursar can get all the staff into work. Mainly it is to talk about developments and what new projects are taking place during the year ahead, then the Headmaster talks about new staff and students joining the college.

When he came home I could tell by his face there was something he had to tell us, normally when he came in it would be remarks like 'another wasted day'. But he just said "let's have tea, then I will tell you the news". After tea Dad came out with it, "We have a celebrity joining the staff on Monday, Roger Royal is going to be our new chaplain". We had all been shocked when in the summer holidays Richard Avery had died suddenly while on holiday with his family. He was only in his forties and had been chaplain for six years, now one of the governors, through people he knew in the city, had managed to bring Roger Royal to the college.

There are many influential people connected with the college and they receive lots of V.I.P. visitors from royalty, showbiz and politicians. Dad had met a lot while working there, he knew that I would be interested in this piece of news. As long as I can remember I had listened to Sunday Half Hour with Roger Royal, even wrote for a hymn to be played one time with no luck. When I was away at boarding school in Gloucester on Sunday evenings all the girls would be listening to *Top Twenty Tunes* but I used to sit in another room and listen to Sunday Half Hour on my own. The other piece of news was that Michael Aspel's son would be a student next term.

On Tuesday whilst at Park Place I went into the chapel, sitting there was Father Maurice, I had known him a long time and could talk to him about anything. He is a very kind and holy person, even now he phones me every Sunday night to see how I am.

As we sat together he said, "have you something on your mind Ann, you seem troubled in some way, not your happy, smiling self?"

"Yes Father," I said, "I keep thinking about my future, I would like to get settled in a home somewhere, then I won't be a burden to my parents".

"Your parents love you and never think you are a burden, but I do know what you mean," he replied.

We sat there a while and said a few prayers together, he then said, "next month I am attending a conference in London and will make some enquiries for you."

A few weeks went by, then one evening when Dad came home he said, "I have a surprise for you Ann, next Saturday, after lessons finish, you are going to meet Roger Royal, Mum will bring you at 11.30". I was quite excited, Dad had told us quite a bit about him, saying in the staff room he always had a story to tell about people he had met while recording his programme.

Roger was not at the college full time, every Wednesday he would be off travelling the country to record his programme which went out on the following Sunday evening. Dad said, "even when he took morning assembly he would stop half way through a hymn telling us we were not singing good enough let's try again."

When I met Roger Royal he was so nice to me, he took me into his room and wanted to know all about me. I found him so easy to talk to, he understood and was very interested in what I had done in my life, saying that I was a very determined young lady. I mentioned that I had asked for a hymn to be played on his programme, but he told me he was sorry, saying that all the requests go to the BBC in London and were nothing to do with him. We must have spent nearly an hour together, I thanked him saying that it had been a very special time for me. Just before I left he said, "Ann don't tell your father, but he is one of the mainstays here in college, I know they are going to miss him when he does retire."

The next time that I saw Father Maurice at Park Place he showed me a piece out of a Catholic paper on Residential Care Homes. One article mentioned a new home opened in Accrington, Lancashire for young physically disabled people. It seemed just what I had been looking for, I thanked him for his help, he said, "take this home and talk it over with your parents Ann before you do anything."

After what had happened before, I knew my Mum would be unlikely to want anything to do with it, so I asked Julie to help me write a letter to the manager asking for details about the home.

Two weeks later Julie showed me a letter which she had received about the home. It was a new purpose-built home in its own grounds on the outskirts of town. There were twelve rooms, one used for respite care, at that time they had only seven residents aged between eighteen and thirty. Teresa the manager suggested as I lived so far away, it would be best if I went on respite care for a month to see if I liked it before deciding what to do.

I knew that now I would have to talk to my parents, and I was not looking forward to that at all. In fact it took me two weeks before I had the courage to face them. Mum was very annoyed with me for going behind their backs, saying, "I thought we had finished with all this moving away from home? I had a good settled life now, why change things?

I tried to explain that I was thinking of my future, I was nearly thirty years old and needed to be settled. Dad would be retiring in a few years and I wanted them to have some time on their own without having to worry about me. In the end Dad agreed saying that he would phone Teresa to arrange a date for my visit.

During the following weeks Mum and I had some good talks, I told her that I was a bit older now and, with all my treatment in Chester, could do more for myself and knew I could cope a lot better with people. Mum said she was only thinking of me and just wanted me to be happy, saying, "Dad and I love you very much and there will always be a home for you here Ann."

I asked Dad where Accrington was? "It is over the border from Yorkshire," he said, "not far from Colne where Mum was born and Grandad Bob used to drive his trains, but it is a long way from Hampshire Ann, it will be a long journey. I think the best thing will be to travel up on Sunday when the roads are quieter and stay overnight somewhere."

The week before I went Mum told me to try and get plenty of rest, you are going on assessment and will have to show them what you can do for yourself. On the Tuesday I went to Park Place and told them I would not see them for a month, Paula and Julie wished me luck, I had my lunch with the Sisters and they all gave me a wonderful send off with special prayers. On Saturday Mum and I had a busy day packing my case and bags, she said, "well my dear, I hope it all works out for you, just remember you are loved and we will always be here for you". She made me my favourite meal of steak and kidney, which was delicious, I thanked them both for being so understanding, telling them I would not let them down. Dad said he wanted to be away by eight o'clock the following morning so we all had an early night.

Mum woke me with a cup of tea and asked me how I felt, I told her that I had slept well, but was just a bit apprehensive about the month ahead. Dad had packed the car telling us the forecast was good so we should have a good journey, he had booked us into a Travel Lodge near Burnley which is only a few miles from Accrington.

We had a good journey, the roads were not too busy so Dad suggested we call at Chester for lunch. He knew it was one of my favourite places with happy memories of Joan and Peter who helped me so much with all their treatment. After a very good lunch and a walk by the river we were off again - Lancashire next stop.

As we came into Accrington next morning Mum asked me if I was nervous, I suppose in a way I was and yet looking forward to seeing the home and people there. A tree lined drive with pretty flowerbeds curved up to the house. A man had just jumped out of a mini bus and came over to our car. He introduced himself, "I am Frank, Teresa's husband, you must be Ann we have been expecting you. Have you had a good journey?" he then opened the door and took us inside the home.

From the lobby there was a very large lounge with two dining tables at one end and armchairs at the other by the television. To one side were patio doors leading onto the garden, at the other side a large conservatory had been built. The residents were having morning coffee, a nice lady came across saying, "I am Joyce one of the care staff, can I get you all a coffee? I will tell Teresa you have arrived. We have been looking forward to meeting you Ann."

Teresa was a tall, slim lady with dark hair and glasses, she came to sit with us. "When you have had your coffee I will take you around the home then we can go into my office and have a talk."

As we went from the lounge there was an open area with a snooker table in the middle, leading from there down both sides there were six rooms, toilets and bathrooms. Teresa showed us the end room on the left, saying, "this will be your room Ann". There was a washbasin in one corner, a large wardrobe with cupboards above, a locker next to the bed and a unit with a television on by the window which looked out over the garden. Both Mum and I were impressed with how the rooms had been set out, there was room for a wheel chair to move round.

After looking round the home we went with Teresa into her office, she told us that the home had been open just over a year and, at the moment, she had seven residents, two men and five ladies. Her aim was to give young people a home they could call their own, where they could be as independent as possible. "During your stay Ann," she said, "we will assess you, Carol my deputy will look after you and help you settle in. We want you to feel like one of the family here. I hope you enjoy your stay and decide to come and share our home." My parents wished me luck and told me to just do my best, "remember we love you and will always be here for you", then they left to travel back to Hampshire.

Teresa then took me and introduced me to the residents, they all told me their names and I soon got to know them. Later a nice young carer called Nicola took me down to my room and helped me unpack. She was very friendly saying she liked working there and hoped I would be happy and decide to stay. She said her mother also worked there and I would see her next week after her holiday. During the evening meal Ann came to sit with me she told me she was the oldest resident and if anyone had any problems they could talk to her and she would try to help them.

Next morning I met Carol, the deputy, she came to my room and introduced herself, she only lived just down the road and was a nurse, she had two young boys and when the home opened she came to work there. Carol asked me in what way I needed help, telling me not to worry just carry on as I would normally, "I will watch you during the week, don't be afraid to ask any of us if you need any help, we want you to be happy here and hope you will stay."

Later that morning at coffee time a nice young man came in with the papers and magazines, all the young ladies had their eyes on him, Rosie said, "That is Sean the handyman/driver, we all fancy him. Sean lived with his mother Peggy in the cottage next door. Peggy was the cook she made excellent meals, and lovely home made puddings to finish with.

Over the next few days I got to know who everyone was. Carol was nice to me, she watched me dress and undress to see what help I needed, also in the bathroom to see if I could manage the bath myself. Although I did need some help I was fortunate because I could walk about in the home on my own, most of the others used a wheel chair.

When the weather was nice Frank, Sean and the staff would take us out in the two mini buses, we went over the moors to Pendle Hill or the Trough of Bowland and stopped for afternoon tea. Sometimes they took us to the coast, Blackpool or Morecambe, it was so good to walk along the seafront we all loved it. At weekends Frank was the cook he made beautiful roast dinners, just like Mum. It felt like one big happy family and I began to think of it as my home. Frank took us to church on Sunday and sometimes we would all go out for a meal afterwards.

Each Monday morning a group of retired ladies came to do crafts with us, they did flower arrangements, sewing and knitting, making things for the summer fair, which was the home's main fundraising event of the year. It was interesting to be with them they were so jolly and full of fun, telling us stories about their lives working in the mills, they called them, 'The good old days' but said it was very hard work, up at six in the morning, working the looms, and no tea breaks in those days. I loved to hear them talk, I had missed that a lot, I remember my Auntie Phylis and Doris telling me stories about their lives.

On Thursdays two volunteers came to play games and do art with us. Sometimes Ann, one of the volunteers, would take me into Accrington to look round the shops. Fridays another lady, Lesley, came to do yoga with us, she ran a group which brought other ladies into the home from the area. This was another way of making friends outside of the home.

A few days later Teresa and Carol had a chat with me to see how I had got on and my feelings about the home. I told them that I felt very happy being there and would like to make it my home. Teresa said I had worked hard and seemed to fit in well with the other residents and offered me a place. I said I would have to talk to my parents to see if they agreed. Teresa said she would phone them, she came back to say Mum and Dad would come up at the weekend and have a meeting, she also said that Mum would contact my social worker in Winchester to see about funding for me.

As soon as Mum came into the home and saw just how happy I was, laughing with my new friends, I think she knew this was the right place for me. I introduced her to my friends they all said, "please let Ann come to live with us, she is such good fun to be with". We had a meeting with Teresa who told them I had worked hard and mixed well with all the residents, she told Mum the room was mine if that was what we wanted. Mum said she had phoned Ann Marie the social worker, telling her about Rough Lee and a placement for me. She said because it was not in Hampshire there would have to be a meeting when I went home regarding the funding. Teresa said she would keep my room for a month and hoped everything worked out. I thanked her for everything and we said we'd keep her informed, then we set off for home.

I did not stop talking during the journey, telling Mum and Dad what I had been doing and about the people I had met. Mum just said, "I know you are excited love and we are glad you like the home and the people there, but it is up to Hampshire now, you will have to try and keep calm and be patient. Ann Marie will do her best for you."

Over the next couple of weeks Ann Marie seemed to spend more and more time with me, there were forms to fill in, phone calls being made then she had to present my case before the full meeting. I was very nervous about the outcome, then one evening we had a phone call about nine o'clock she told us that Social Services had agreed to fund me. It would take about two weeks for all the paper work to be done but we could let Teresa know I could start next month. I thanked her for all the help she had given me, she said that she would call to see me before I left home.

Chapter Seventeen

Now it hit me, this was a very big step that I was taking, not only leaving home, but moving 250 miles away from my parents and many friends, in my heart I knew I had made the right decision, but it was scary. I sat down with Mum and Dad and we made a list of things to be done and people to see, maybe some for the very last time.

I did not realise just how many friends I had made in the twelve years I had been in Alresford. It is a very friendly little town and word soon got around that I was leaving. Nearly all the shopkeepers came to have a word with us as we went by, even my doctor called across the road, "you must come and see me before you go Ann". It took Mum and I twice as long to do the shopping with people stopping us to have a chat. Mum said, "you are a very popular young lady, won't you miss all this?"

"Yes Mum," I said. "I will very much, but I have to make a break now or I might regret it later."

Mum was very good, she phoned round lots of my friends inviting them for afternoon tea, we seemed to have visitors nearly every day. Nancy Hill and some of the Faith and Light group in Winchester, Bob who had helped me so much and our dear friend Margaret. She has always been there for me with sound advice or listening to my troubles or problems. I think it hit me how lucky I had been to have people to support me like this. Did I deserve it? I know there have been times when I have been a horrible person, to Mum and Dad especially.

Dad arranged for us to visit Sister Felicity in London. We first met eighteen years ago in Lourdes, she has always been good to me and given us all advice when we needed it. Of course we had to meet Mother Superior she gave us her blessing and said we were always in her prayers. Sister said, just before we left, "you have come a long way since I first saw you Ann, as a very demanding teenager, now you are a young lady I am very proud to know you, please keep in touch." I think we were both upset at saying goodbye. I told her I would never forget her and thanked her for being my friend.

Unbeknown to me, Mum had arranged a party for me at Park Place on my last Tuesday, it was such a surprise. Father Maurice came from Basingstoke and Father Andrew with all the Sisters, Paula, Julie and Meg from the bookshop. I just did not know what to say. Father Maurice took me in the chapel for a chat telling me he would phone me every Sunday evening and if I needed him anytime I could phone him. "I hope everything works out for you Ann you deserve this, it is now another phase of your life beginning, so make the most of it." Everyone came out to see me off when Dad picked me up at teatime, they wished me luck and told me to keep in touch.

As the weekend came nearer we packed my clothes and sorted out other things I had to take. Dad had made me a corner unit for my room like a desk to put my TV and typewriter on. He had hired a van for the journey because I had so much to take. Mum and I had some lovely talks, I felt close to her and said, "I know you only want the best for me Mum and I do appreciate everything you have done for me all these years." She just said, "Ann, my love just remember you are loved so much".

Because Dad was busy at college he told us we would have to set off early in the morning, and come straight back when they had settled me in. So we were all up at six a.m. and away by seven, even though it was early a few of our neighbours were there to wave me off.

We had a good journey up the motorway and arrived in Accrington in time for lunch, the residents were very pleased to see me again and had made me a poster with, 'Welcome to your new home Ann' on the main door. Straight after lunch Mum and Dad unpacked all my things, Mum sorted all my clothes out for me, while Dad fixed my unit and got my TV and typewriter working. Another surprise was to see a telephone in my room. I did not know, but Mum had asked Teresa if I could have one. She said with them being so far away they would not be able to visit as much as they'd like. Luckily Teresa had agreed, as long as my parents paid the bills.

By four o'clock everything was sorted out, Frank made Mum and Dad something to eat then it was time for us to say our goodbyes. I gave Mum and Dad a big hug and thanked them for all they had done for me. Mum said she would phone next day to let me know they had got home OK then they set off for Hampshire while I started my new life in Lancashire.

It did not hit me straightaway what I had done, I was thirty years old and had just left home. Now it was up to me what I made of my life here at Rough Lee.

During the summer months life was good, if we did not go out for the day we would sit on the patio. The staff kept us refreshed with big jugs of juice and ice cream. Being only eight of us, we were like one big family.

Early in September a lady called from Accrington College, she told us that they were now running courses for people with disabilities and wondered if we would be interested. Teresa asked her to leave us a prospectus to study together then she would get in touch with her. There were various things on offer, most of the courses being very basic, but they looked interesting so we decided to enrol. Not everyone chose the same things to do, I decided to try computer studies, basic cookery, health and hygiene and drama. Some of us would be going in the morning and some in the afternoon. I was looking forward to starting, meeting people and making new friends.

I soon realised how limited I was with my hand movements, finding the cookery especially difficult as I could only use my left hand. Luckily there were many volunteers to help us. I had watched Mum at home, she enjoyed cooking and baking so I knew what to do but I couldn't put it into practice. The tutors were very good and understanding, telling me to do as much as I could then ask the staff for any help I needed.

With Mum being a nurse she had talked a lot to me about her training in hospitals, how hard it was and how strict the Sister was. She told me how they had to do the menial work as well as the medical but that she'd enjoyed it all the same. So I was very interested in the health and hygiene course. Even if I could not do the practical side, I could tell the staff what should be done and I got very good marks. Dad had always told me I liked showing off so the drama group suited me and we had lots of fun together and I made a lot of new friends.

Mum and Dad would phone me each week to see how I was and to tell me their news about things down south. I kept in touch with most of my friends by phone, hoping that my phone bill wouldn't be too large! I did miss seeing Mum and Dad very much, but I never told them that I was homesick as I did not want to worry them. It had been my own doing so I knew that I should make the most of it and try to make this my home now.

With going to college and the darker evenings we did not go out as much, usually just on Sunday for a meal which we all looked forward to. Soon we began to prepare for Christmas, this would be my first Christmas away from home, another new experience for me. Mum and Dad told me that they were coming up to stay in the guest room at Elsie's flat in Bingley for a few days over Christmas and would come to see me. Frank said he would get us a real Christmas tree this year, then plant it in the garden and try to keep it for each year. Teresa told us she had booked seats to see 'Cinderella', my favourite pantomime so we were looking forward to that. When I was little my aunties Phyllis and Doris would always take me to the pantomime either in Leeds or Bradford. Doris used to get as excited as the children, shouting and joining in the singing with the actors.

We all helped to decorate the tree and put streamers and balloons all over the lounge. Sean fixed fairy lights on the tree for us and everything looked lovely. Frank was a good cook and he made us a smashing Christmas lunch, roast turkey with all the trimmings and Christmas pudding, we even had a glass of wine. With carols playing on the record player we were like one big family together. We thanked Teresa and Frank for looking after us and giving us such a good time. Then we sat around the tree and Frank handed out our presents while we watched the Queen on TV giving her Christmas speech.

Mum and Dad phoned in the morning to wish me Happy Christmas, and to say that they were coming over on Boxing Day to take me out. It was lovely to see them again, they both gave me a big hug telling me that I looked very well. Teresa told them that I had settled in and was working hard at college. They thanked her for looking after me and asked if they could take me out for the day. Dad said although it was cold it was a bright sunny day, "if you wrap up well, how would you like a trip to Blackpool?" He knew that was my favourite place as we had spent many happy holidays there with Grandad Bob. Dad said it was nearly twenty years since we were there and wondered if it had changed at all.

What a lovely day we had, walking along the seafront and watching the tide come in, there were quite a lot of people about. Then we found a restaurant for lunch, I had lots to tell them about my friends and what I was doing at college. Mum kept looking at me and giving me hugs, saying how much she missed me and how she was always thinking about me being so far away. We had a smashing meal then we looked around the shops before returning to Rough Lee. I had really enjoyed being with Mum and Dad again, it was just like old times.

They came again on the Saturday and we went into Burnley to do some shopping. I needed new shoes which always seemed to take ages to choose, but it was nice to spend time with my Mum, I did miss her so much, although I would never tell her, she would only worry about me.

The hardest part was saying our goodbyes. They both gave me a hug and a kiss saying they would see me again at Easter, telling me to work hard and look after myself.

I must admit I felt sad when they left and cried myself to sleep that night in bed, thinking of all the happy times at home with family and friends. My childhood had been so wonderful, always fun, laughter and nice things happening to me. It's only now, as I have listened to some of the residents talking, some have no parents or families that don't want to know, that I realise how lucky I have been.

Early in the new year a lady came to see me called Avril, she told me she went to the Faith and Light group in Lancaster and their leader had been asked to contact me by Nancy Hill, the leader of

Winchester group which I used to attend.

Avril was a lovely person, full of life. She told me they lived in Rishton about five miles away and had adopted a disabled boy called Daniel, they also took in short term foster children. She told me that I could go in their mini bus with them to the Faith and Light meetings in Lancaster and we became good friends. Sometimes I would go to their house for tea after we had been out, Tom, her husband, was always making me laugh, kidding me about the football teams we supported.

Chapter Eighteen

Over the next few months more people were coming for interviews for placement and by the end of the summer our numbers had increased to thirteen and the home was full. Among the new residents were two partially sighted girls, Dawn and Sharon, and also another boy, Kevin, whose parents had died within a short time of each other. He reminded me of Andrew, the boy who had lived near me when we started school.

Teresa and Frank arranged to take us to a farm campsite for a week's holiday during the summer. We were to go in groups of four or five at a time, which made a nice break for us. There was also a caravan in Morecambe which we used for long weekend breaks. There was a social club on the site so after we had been out during the day we could relax and enjoy an evening's entertainment.

Mum used to write me long letters every week which I looked forward to receiving. I could tell she missed me by the way she wrote, we have always had a very special relationship between us and seemed to know how each other felt. I never let on how much I missed her, she would have only worried.

My parents would come up to see me when Dad was on holiday from the college, but they could only stay a few days at a time in Bingley. I was always glad to see them and enjoyed going out for the day with them, especially if they took me over to Yorkshire to visit my friends and our relations. It was always hard saying goodbye when it was time for them to go back home.

Although basically I had settled here and was fairly happy, I had a few misgivings; sometimes I felt very lonely and on my own. I think the main reason was because my parents had always treated me as a normal person with a slight disability, not a disabled person full stop. They had made sure that I had lived as normal a life as possible and everyone around us had treated me the same, here I was just another resident in the home.

|Over the next year I seemed to feel changes taking place with my body, I did not understand what was happening to me, sometimes I would just fall backwards without knowing it was happening. At home I could have told Mum, because she was a nurse, I always knew she would explain medical things to me so that I could understand them. I did tell the staff but they just told me to use my wheelchair more.

Dad's next holiday was Easter, when they came to see me my Mum said, "Ann, we have been doing some serious thinking since our last visit, about when Dad retires next year." She told me that she could not settle down to retirement knowing I was living nearly three hundred miles away, "it's too far to travel, especially as we get older."

So they were going to move nearer to me, I just gave them both a big hug. It was the best news I could have had, to know they would be closer to me again.

During their stay Dad took us on a tour around the area looking at different locations. He called in a few estate agents for details of new developments being built to get some idea of where to live.

Not long after they had gone back home I had a letter from Mum saying that things were happening faster than they'd imagined. Apparently, she had been telling one of her friends about coming back up north when Dad retired and word got around, within a couple of weeks a man called to see them saying he had heard they were going to move. He was looking for a house in Alresford and was interested in ours, he would pay the asking price and it would be in cash, no hold up with chain buying. The one big snag was that he wanted it now, not in a year's time, after a lot of discussion they came to some agreement.

It was too good an opportunity for them to miss, it was decided they would buy a house in Lancashire and move during the summer holidays. Mum would live there by herself and Dad could stay with their friends, Joan and Joe in Holy Bourne, near the college for his last year.

I was so pleased to hear this news, it would mean I could see more of my parents again. Don't get me wrong, I knew it had been the right decision to move into a residential home, because my parents would not always be there for me. I did not want to live on my own in a flat and have to rely on carers coming in each day. I have spoken with a lot of disabled people my age, listening to their stories about care in the community and how they coped.

This was a busy time for my parents so I kept quiet about my own problems, some of the staff were very good and encouraged me in what I was doing, but now I could look forward to talking to my Mum for advice about my health. We had a few trips out in the fine weather and also the short breaks at the caravan in Morecambe and the farm holiday after we finished college for the summer.

Mum kept me informed with things at home, the man buying the house was interested in the furniture also, so they would not need the removal men. Dad said a friend would hire a van and drive up with them, unload then return the same day. So a date was fixed for the end of July to leave about seven a.m., and be in Lancashire for lunchtime.

As the time past I could not wait to see their bungalow in Blackburn. Mum phoned me on the Sunday evening to let me know everything had gone smoothly. The first thing would be to go shopping for furniture, all they had brought with them was the bed, two small chairs, cooking utensils and personal things. So it was a nice surprise when they called in to see me on the Wednesday evening, it had only been four months but seemed much longer since I had last seen them. They told me about the furniture they had bought so far. Dad said he had a lot of work to do, fitting wardrobes, cupboards and shelves everywhere, he wanted to do as much as he could before going back so Mum would be alright on her own. He also wanted to get a bedroom ready for me so that I could maybe spend a weekend with her, it would be good company for her as they did not know anyone yet.

On Sunday afternoon Dad called to pick me up and took me back for tea, it was like old times, Mum's Sunday tea of salmon sandwiches and trifle. The bungalow was on the outskirts of Blackburn and from the front you could see across the countryside and hills.

Mum told me there were some shops nearby, as well as a doctors, chemist and small library, all within walking distance. She had put her special touch on things already telling me she felt very happy about the move and her bungalow saying, "Ann, I knew within a few weeks of being so far away from you that I would never be happy down south again."

Just before it was time for Dad to travel back to college he had a talk with Teresa about my spending a weekend with Mum. She agreed saying I could have every other weekend, either Frank or Sean could take me on Friday afternoon and Mum would bring me back on Sunday evening.

They now had the telephone installed so I could phone Mum or she would ring me during the week, and the weekend I did not go home, she came to Accrington on the Saturday afternoon. I think Mum was settling in well, she said both neighbours were very friendly and she was not frightened of living on her own. My Dad came up once a month for a long weekend, arriving in time for tea on Friday then leaving about five a.m., Monday morning. He said the headmaster was giving him extra time off, if he made up for it during the week.

It was good to have Mum around again, she would take me into town to look around the shops, always buying me little treats. I think it also gave me a bit more confidence knowing she was not too far away. I had not mentioned my falls at all, but one time while at home I just fell backwards. Mum asked if I had lost my balance, but I did not even know I was falling. She sat me down and had a good talk about how long it had been happening and how often, also what was being done about it.

I told her that the staff knew about my falls and they had just said, "It is because of your handicap, if you don't feel well use your wheelchair."

Mum was very upset about that, we as a family have worked so hard over the years to get me where I am now. I asked her what to do and she told me to keep a note of each fall, how often they occurred and the time of day, then we would decide what would happen next. Over the next few weeks I carried on as usual with my life, going to college and being with my friends but also keeping a record each time I fell backwards.

I was looking forward to Christmas this year. Dad had three

weeks holiday, so I was going home for ten days over Christmas and the New Year. This is a special time for us, with my birthday in December. Going to midnight Mass, the church full and the choir singing to welcome the birth of Our Lord, it always gives me a lovely feeling inside. Listening to the scripture readings I can imagine it all taking place all those years ago. Unfortunately it seems to me more people look on Christmas as just a time for parties and over indulging in food and drink than the true meaning.

I had another fall while at home, we sat down and I showed them the notes I had made. There was no regular pattern, it seemed to happen randomly without warning. Mum said, "First I will have a talk with Doctor Ridgway here and ask his advice."

He suggested we contacted Mr Tidswell at the hospital in Blackburn, he was the top neurologist there.

We were fortunate and managed to get a private appointment with him before my Dad had to return to college. Mum and Dad picked me up from the home telling Teresa about the appointment. Mr Tidswell was a kind man, putting me at ease, asking me questions about the falls. He carried out some tests on me and after a while said that my falls were nothing to do with my disability, he wanted to do more tests and also an ECG. Over the next months I saw Mr Tidswell three or four times.

Unfortunately I did not realise that, with my parents taking me to see the specialist, it would cause problems for me at the home. It was as if we had done something wrong, when all we wanted was to find the cause of my falls, poor Mum had to take most of the backlash.

This was the year that Blackburn Rovers won the Premiership title, there was great excitement everywhere. When I was home on Saturday and Blackburn were playing at Ewood, we could hear the loud cheers in our bungalow, especially when it was Alan Shearer scoring a goal. Dad bought me a Rover's scarf to wear, Kevin is a Burnley supporter and Nicola a Liverpool fan so there is lots of friendly banter going on between us.

During the summer my tummy began to give me some problems, I also had very heavy swollen breasts. The staff knew but just told me that it was women's problems, "everyone gets like that at times, you have to put up with it." By the end of the week I was in so much pain I phoned Mum at home. When she came to see me on the Saturday she was shocked to find me laying on my bed in such pain. She sat with me all afternoon telling me to try and rest and that she would phone Doctor Turner on the Monday and she would be here to see him. I think he was concerned when he saw me on Monday and put me on medication straightaway.

The next time I went home Mum asked me if I wanted to come and live back at home, but I told her I was determined to fight for my independence at Rough Lee. We were now looking forward to my Dad retiring in July and planning a surprise party for him, it was also their fortieth wedding anniversary. I asked Mum where she would like to go and she told me to book a table at 'Bentley Wood' for the Saturday evening.

It was so good to see Dad again, I hoped to persuade him to take Mum on holiday. She did not look well at all and I felt happier now he would be there for her all the time. We had a lovely evening, the meal was very good, as we sat talking Dad told us about his last week at college, the leaving parties and presentations from both students and colleagues. He said he found it hard saying farewell after twenty years, especially when the headmaster gave him such a glowing send off in front of everyone at the final prize giving assembly. I know he was well liked, they thought highly of him at Treloars for his hard work and dedication.

When Dad took me back on Sunday night, I asked if he would take Mum on holiday. I told him she worries about me at the home, but I can cope, he promised to do as I asked. He phoned me in the week to say he'd had a good talk with Mum, she did not want to go far but would welcome a short break in Morecambe, so they would go at the weekend for a few days.

It was the August bank holiday weekend the next time I went home to stay, I was so pleased to see Mum looking healthier after their little holiday. While we were having tea on Friday evening they asked me if I fancied going to St. Anne's next day? I said,

"Oh, yes please." We had some lovely holidays there when I was very young, Fairhaven Lake and the green where I took my first steps trying to walk.

I woke early next morning with terrific pains in my very swollen tummy, my head ached and I was sweating, I wanted to get out of bed but I was frightened of falling so I called for Mum. As soon as she saw me she said, "don't worry love, just lay there. Dad will take us straight to the hospital." I was so glad to be home with Mum and Dad.

A lady doctor examined me and asked lots of questions, after a while she told Mum they were going to admit me so that they could carry out further tests. While in hospital I saw a gynaecologist who explained everything to us, apparently the heavy periods were the cause and they were also connected to the falls I was having. I was put on some different tablets to slow my periods down and was told to go back to the clinic in three months. Since then my general health has improved and I have not had any more falls. I feel like I have been given a fresh start in life.

One Saturday while out shopping in Blackburn with my parents, we came across a display of work by students at the local college. Staff were on hand answering questions about the various courses and handing out the new prospectus for the coming year, encouraging people to enrol. We took one home to look through, Dad was looking for something new to try for himself but Mum was very interested in a new course, Creative writing for beginners. "How would you fancy that Ann?" she asked me, "I am sure you will enjoy it, have I to contact the college and inquire for you?"

I remembered Margaret coming to take me for English lessons, we had done a little writing which I had enjoyed. Mum found out the details and when she explained about my disability they said it would not be a problem and that I could have support with me. Dad said he was going to sign up for the wood carving course so would enrol for me at the same time.

I stopped college in Accrington and just went to Blackburn on Wednesdays. Dad would take me then collect me at 3.30pm. I'd have a meal with them then back in the evening. When I arrived the first week Joyce, the tutor, who was a dark haired lady with spectacles introduced me to Val, my support worker.

Val was a lovely blonde lady who was very bubbly, we seemed to get on straightaway, she was always making me laugh, I was frightened it might get me into trouble but no-one minded. All the group were very friendly and supportive, I was the only disabled student and the youngest, but they accepted me as a normal person which pleased me.

Joyce would talk about different aspects of writing, how to build a story together, the different ways to interpret events, I found it very interesting indeed. She would set us homework, giving us a title then asking us to write about 250 words on the subject. Val and I would talk about it then she would write a rough outline for me which I would then work on at home on my typewriter. As my speech is not too good, Joyce read out my story for me, hearing the other students and seeing how they wrote helped me a lot. Sometimes the discussions became very animated and Joyce had to step in, being treated as one of the group with no special privileges gave me a good feeling inside.

Chapter Nineteen

My life had improved again, it was nice going to church with my parents on Sundays, going to college on my own and enjoying my work. Then early in the New Year I had a lovely surprise, my friend Paula wrote telling me about the changes being made at Park Place. They were making two rooms totally independent for disabled visitors to stay and had invited me down for a holiday.

This was wonderful news, I have spent many happy days there and called it 'my second home' and Sister Evelyn 'my second mum', we have been friends for years. Once the dates were fixed I made arrangement for as many of my friends as possible to come and see me. It would be my first holiday on my own. I could hardly contain my excitement or concentrate on my college work. Paula had arranged with my father that she would come up for me, stay with friends in Upholland overnight, collect me then travel back. Dad would bring me home again, it would save him doing both journeys.

I could not wait for the first week in May and the start of my holiday. Paula arrived about 11am, Mum made us tea and sandwiches while Dad put my things in her car. My parents thanked Paula for taking me, gave me a big hug, telling me to enjoy my holiday, they had no qualms about my going on my own, knowing the Sisters would look after me.

The journey down was good, but what a surprise as we arrived at Park Place, a banner saying 'Ann Welcome Home' hung over the main doorway. Then a big embrace from all the Sisters as they came out to greet me, I was so overwhelmed. They gave me a wonderful holiday, looking after me and all my many visitors. What fun Sister Evelyn had showering me every morning, in the end she came in dressed in a rain coat and Wellingtons, we could not stop laughing.

Paula took me for days out, sometimes Amelia would come with us, it was lovely seeing old friends again, catching up with all the news. My very dear friend Father Maurice spent the day with me, he had phoned every Sunday since I moved and been a great help to me. Being with the Sisters, joining in Mass in their little chapel, brought the yearning I'd had from years back of becoming a nun. I know and acknowledge that it will never happen because of my disability, but still I felt something was missing in my life.

I mentioned this to Paula one day when she took me hospital visiting in Portsmouth, later at her house she showed me a missal that had belonged to her mother, it was for 'The Third Order of Carmel'. Paula told me her mother had belonged to the Order most of her life, it was for laypeople who wanted to live a more dedicated religious life. I was very interested to learn more about the Order and Paula said she would write to the Carmelite Centre in Aylesford asking them to send details to me.

All too soon my holiday was coming to an end. My Dad was coming down to collect me, staying with Margaret in Winchester overnight, then coming to Park Place in the morning. I could not thank the Sisters and Paula enough for giving me such a wonderful time, I think the Sisters had enjoyed me being with them. They all came outside to wave us off asking me to come again next year. I shouted "JUST TRY AND STOP ME!"

I did not stop talking all the way home, telling Dad what I had been doing and who had called to see me. He just looked at me saying, "I don't have to ask if you have enjoyed yourself, it is written on your face." I spent the weekend at home, Mum could not get over how much I had changed. I told her this holiday was just what I needed, to spend time in the chapel on my own, but also talking to Father Maurice and the Sisters, it had given me a new outlook on life.

I had only been back home a few weeks when one evening one of the staff came into my room saying there were two visitors to see me. A lady and a younger man came in and introduced themselves saying, "I am Marilyn and this is Damian." They were from the Blackburn Chapter Third Order Carmel. Marilyn said they had been giving my address from Aylesford who asked them to contact me. They sat with me a while talking about the Order. Damian was the leader at Blackburn, he lived on his own, he had a slight disability but said he coped very well. Before they left we said some prayers together then they gave me some booklets to read about the Order, inviting me to attend their next meeting in Blackburn.

During my next long weekend at home, I showed my parents the booklets on Carmel. Mum said, "Right Ann, tomorrow we will go to St. Anne's, sit on the green and read through them together." I could see Mum was interested when she read them. I trusted her advice impeccably so was pleased when she told me, "Ann, I think this could be for you my love. Take it slowly and see how it works out."

The Blackburn Chapter meets on the third Saturday of the month at St. Joseph's Church, I felt a bit nervous when my Dad took me to the meeting but Marilyn introduced me and made me feel welcome. There were about fifteen people and a priest who gave a talk then we moved into the church for Mass and special Carmel prayers, then back into the room for tea and biscuits during which one or two people came to talk to me. Father Martin came up from Cheltenham for the meetings. He was a small, friendly man, he said he was pleased to meet me and hoped I'd find something in the scriptures to help me.

After I had attended another two meetings, Marilyn asked me if I would like to be received into the Order? She told me once you have been received you study the rules and Carmel scriptures for two years then you take a vow and be professed. So at the next meeting Mum and Dad came to the Mass and saw me being received into The Third Order of Carmel. After Mass everyone came to congratulate me on taking my first step, I could tell Mum was proud of me, standing on my own at the altar being received. Marilyn used to come up once a month to give me some instruction, sometime Roland, her husband, came as well they lived in Nelson and we became good friends.

I was enjoying my creative writing at college joining in the discussions in class and making more friends. The only change being Val had left, but Joyce said, "You don't need a support worker Ann, if you sit by me I can keep my eye on you." That made me feel more independent.

While at home over Christmas I noticed how tired Mum was, in the evening while we were watching television within ten minutes she could be fast asleep. When I mentioned this to Dad he said, "I know love, I have tried to get Mum to go to the doctor but she won't, she just says 'leave me alone, I am alright.'"

So it came as a surprise when she told us she would like to go to Llandudno together and have a family holiday. I was so pleased and thought it would be lovely for us to go together. As I was going to Park Place in May, I asked them to try and book it for early July before all the schools broke up.

I only had a week at Park Place this year, Sister Evelyn was spending more time away now, so we had to fit in with her as she liked to look after me. The Sisters told me how much better I had become, more independent and my speech had improved, they gave me a lovely holiday.

I look on this as my retreat where I can spend quiet time in the chapel reflecting on my life, thanking God for the many blessings bestowed on me. I had a lot to pray for this year with my Carmel and being worried about Mum. Father Maurice was pleased I had joined the Carmel, saying he would pray for me at Mass, the Sisters were also keeping me in their prayers.

When I got home Mum had booked the holiday. I would have my own room which was a nice surprise. The hotel was right on the seafront, quite posh!! We had a wonderful week favoured by the weather and smashing food. I think that I amazed Mum by being so independent in my own room. It was lovely just walking on the promenade together, watching families playing on the beach, the blue sea and sky. Mum and I did a lot of talking, she seemed to want me with her to reassure her that I was happy now at Rough Lee. I told her my life had never been more settled, everything was going well for me now.

The next day Dad took me up Great Orme on the little railway, I mentioned this to him. He said, "I know what you mean love, she keeps asking me if I think you are happy." He told me not to worry. "Mum loves you very much, it is just her way and she cannot help herself."

I had seen a poster for a symphony concert, music by Mozart,

Strauss and from the Proms. I knew Mum would love it so I treated them on our last night. What a wonderful evening we had, Dad had booked a taxi to the theatre, the orchestra was brilliant and everyone enjoyed themselves. We walked back to the hotel along the promenade with fairy lights shining above and the sound of the tide coming in.

A perfect end to our holiday.

Chapter Twenty

The following week I was surprised to receive a letter from Mum, one which I read often and will treasure all my life. I feel that I must enclose it in my story.

To our dear Ann,
First we want to say what a wonderful holiday you helped us to have. I can never remember dad and I being so proud of you and we have been so many times over the years.

These few days together have given us so much happiness and made us realise you have a future at last Ann, and whatever happens, I am sure now your dreams and prayers will be answered. You are accepted and treated as a normal person by everyone – with only a slight handicap. What an achievement to have your own room and be so independent – I think both of us are redundant! This was a great achievement for you Ann.

Thank you for taking us to the theatre, you made it special for us Ann, and the happiness you radiate to others stands out. You gave the lady behind us so much pleasure as you have done to so many people over the years, right from being young – you helped Grandad Bob fill a big gap in his life after Grandma died – when I look back over your young life, with your lovely smile and now with your caring and loving attitude and thinking of others instead of feeling sorry for yourself, we can't express in words how we feel.

We do know you will continue, this gift you have been given from above. Over the years you have worked hard and it's given me so much pleasure to help you through it. I don't think there is a happier mum anywhere, and dad is proud to be your dad – he may not say much but he loves you.

I know you will continue to work and achieve your goals in life. Our Lady will help you Ann. Being a Carmalite is for you, you have all the attributes to be in the order.

Be happy always love, you will always have our love and support,
the bad times are over. Just be yourself always, never change.
We love you dearly.
Mum and Dad xxx

I have been blessed to have the most wonderful parents anyone could wish for, it is only with their boundless love and devotion that I am the person I am today and I want everyone to know.

~*~

On our return to college after the summer break, Joyce asked us all to write a short piece about our early life. It was very interesting listening to the different stories. During our discussion someone asked me what my earliest memories were. I thought a while then said going on holiday to Filey, my aunties came to look after me so that my parents could just relax, I would have been about eighteen mouths old. They seemed surprised that I could remember so far back, I said I have always had a good memory. Joyce said, "why don't you write your autobiography Ann, ask your parents about the early part and build from there. It will take you a long time but well worth the effort. Over the last four or five years I've put on paper the story of my life, I think I have kept all the group enthralled.

Among the many cards and letters I received for my birthday was one from Sister Felicity in London which caused me some concern. We met in Lourdes about twenty years ago and I used to phone her every month until her hearing deteriorated so now we wrote instead. She told me she had been in hospital with breathing problems, I mentioned this to Mum, who thought very highly of Sister, and she said we should make the effort to visit in the New Year.

It was while staying at home over Christmas that Mum had a very bad fit of coughing and trouble getting her breath. She insisted on cooking but would then spend the afternoon in bed. Both Dad and I were worried about her but she would not have the doctor, only saying how sorry she was for upsetting our Christmas. I was very concerned about her but she insisted there was nothing to worry about and carried on as normal.

Dad promised me he would look after Mum and make sure she took things easier, saying she had led a very hard life helping others, it was now time to help her.

About a month into the New Year Mum began thinking about going to London to visit Sister Felicity, saying, "She's getting old, I don't want to wait too long." Dad thought it was to early for Mum to do all that travelling but she insisted she was feeling better. After much talking it was decided we would travel down early Sunday morning, visit Sister in the afternoon, stay in a Travel Lodge near Winchester a couple of nights then see other friends.

Dad would arrange the Travel Lodge booking and I would write to Sister and also Father Maurice to see if we could meet on the Monday. We were lucky, the weather was good for the journey, Mum was wrapped up well in the back of the car with a flask of coffee and would nod off occasionally but otherwise everything went all right. After a couple of stops and getting through London traffic we arrived about 2.00pm

Sister Felicity was very pleased to see us, making a nice cup of tea first then she told us she had arranged a hot meal, phoning through for them to bring it for us. It was lovely seeing her again after nearly six years. She asked how I was and about joining the Carmel, "When you are professed Ann, you will wear the brown scapula like we do." I could tell that she was pleased for me. Mum asked about her health and she told us that the doctors got her stabilized in hospital and put her on medication which was helping, although she soon got out of breath.

After a most welcome meal we were shown into the parlour to see 'Mother' as all the Sisters called her. We were accustomed to this routine now but still found it strange seeing Mother sat behind an iron grill. She had always taken a keen interest in me and my progress over the years, Sister Felicity had shown them all my stories I had written. All too soon it was time for us to go, Sister usually gives me a good talking to when I see her but today she told me. "Ann, for the first time I can see that you are settled, so different from the restless girl I first met, I am proud of you for taking the first step into Carmel." Coming from Sister that meant a great deal to me. We said our goodbyes and I said I would keep in touch then we left for Winchester.

We had arranged to see Father Maurice at eleven o'clock the next morning at the church in Alton, the diocesan priests were having a meeting there. Father took us into the sitting room for coffee while we talked, it was so nice to see him again. He has been one of my mainstays from the first time we met, always there in my hour of need with helpful advice or just to listen to me get things off my chest. We talk on the phone every week, he is not just a priest, but a special, dear friend. It was nice for my parents to meet him again too.

We went for some lunch after leaving Father Maurice, but halfway through the meal, Mum began another coughing bout and had to rush to the toilet where she was violently ill. Once Dad had got her settled again he said the best thing would be to make our way home. He phoned the Travel Lodge to cancel our room then we began our journey home, luckily we had no hold ups on the roads so we made good time. Mum promised to see the doctor the next day, after she'd had some toast she went to bed.

I asked Dad to take me to Rough Lee, I knew he was worried about Mum and with me out of the way he could concentrate on looking after her. I phoned the following evening and Dad told me the doctor had given Mum a thorough examination and he suspected migraine to be the cause. He put her on medication and said he would see her again in a month. I was pleased there was nothing too seriously wrong and told Dad I would see them at the weekend.

The next time Marilyn came to see me she asked me how I felt about the order, saying, "I have talked to most of our Chapter and everyone agrees that you should be ready to take your vows soon. We are having a special Mass at our July meeting, that would be a lovely time for you to be professed. She asked me to think about it. I knew I had worked hard to follow the scriptures and felt that I was a better person, but was that enough? Of course I wanted to be professed and thanked Marilyn for everything she had done for me.

Towards the end of May when Dad took me to college he seemed quiet and pre-occupied, I asked if anything was wrong but he just said he would tell me after class. When he collected me he told me that Mum was in hospital, she had had a terrific headache, was violently sick and coughing up blood. When he left the hospital, they were taking her for a scan.

Mum looked so ill just lying still in bed. The nurse told us the scan showed a cerebral haemorrhage and they might have to operate. They arranged to move her to a special unit in Preston and we stayed with Mum until the ambulance came. I gave her a kiss saying I would see her at the weekend, then Dad took me back to Rough Lee. He told the staff there about Mum and asked them to keep an eye on me, then he left for Preston, saying he would keep me informed on her progress. He told me not to worry too much. Next day when he phoned, he said the doctors were trying Mum on drugs first to see if they would halt the bleeding, she had to lay still and not move her head. I went to see her at the weekend, she looked a little better, I sat holding her hand and she was talking very quietly to me saying, "Don't worry Ann, I will soon be well again."

Mum had been in Preston two weeks, it was the Spring Bank holiday and Dad said I could have a long weekend at home. I was pleased to see Mum looking brighter, she was propped up with pillows, talking and saying she was hungry. The nurse told me Mum had responded to the drugs and the doctors were pleased with her progress. As we were leaving on the Sunday, she wanted to come home with us and get some fish and chips. The nurse just said, "maybe next time the doctor sees you, he will let you go home."

I was woken next morning by the sound of the telephone ringing, I could hear Dad talking, it was still dark outside. He came into my room saying that the hospital had rung to say that Mum had collapsed with a massive head bleed and that she was in intensive care. It was only five a.m., but we got ready and were there within the hour. A porter showed us the way to ICU and a nurse took us into the waiting room, telling us that the doctors were still with Mum but they would see us when they'd finished.

We seemed to sit there ages, another family were waiting also, their daughter had been in a car accident and was badly injured. At last a nurse came and took Dad in to see Mum for a short time. When he came back, he told me it was very serious and I would have to be brave when I went in. He said there were tubes and drains with machines all around her and she was on life support. The doctors were trying to stabilize her before they did anything else. When at last they let me in, I was too frightened to look, you see this kind of thing on TV but when it's your own mum... I just burst into tears when I saw her.

The nurse was very kind to me saying it looked a lot worse than it really was. They put a chair so I could sit and just hold her hand. Her head was all bandaged and tubes were coming out everywhere. They let me sit for half an hour then I had to leave, this went on all day. My Dad phoned Rough Lee from the hospital to let them know he was keeping me at home and we stayed at the hospital until eight that evening but not much changed.

The following day they took Mum for a scan, when the doctor had seen the results he wanted to see Dad in his office. He told him the scan showed bleeding and they would have to operate, the operation was scheduled for twelve noon the next day. The nurse said if I went in the morning I could see Mum before they took her down to theatre at 11.30am. They explained it would be a long operation but to phone about six o'clock as they would know more then. It was very interesting watching them get Mum ready for theatre, but also upsetting. She had not spoken to me since asking for fish and chips. I kissed her forehead as they wheeled her away.

That was one of the worst days of my life, we could not settle at home and did not want to eat anything. It seemed to take ages for the clock to move to six but when it did Dad phoned the hospital. The nurse told him that she had just returned, by the time we got to the hospital she was settled in again. When we went into ICU there seemed to be more tubes then ever coming out of Mum and the doctor wanted to see Dad straightaway.

When he returned to me in the waiting room he told me the doctors could not do what they had hoped. When they had operated on her head, the rupture was too near the main part of the brain, it would have been too dangerous. They packed it to try and stop the bleeding but they didn't know how successful it would be.

Mum was in ICU ten more days, just laying still, being fed by tubes and kept alive by the life support. I asked Dad if that was how Auntie Doris had been after she was stabbed, he said, "Yes love, that is why I did not want you to see her." After another scan they moved Mum onto Ward 2A. She was the only patient in the room and a nurse sat with her all the time.

Chapter Twenty One

There was a good restaurant at Preston, when I was home at weekends, we would go there after Mass for our roast lunch then sit with Mum until 6pm, after tea I'd go back to Rough Lee. Poor Dad, I felt sorry for him seeing Mum every day like that, she could not talk or move, but just lay still in bed. He would phone me every night to keep me informed of any progress. After a week on Ward 2A they took the tubes out to see how she would respond, but she got very distressed so it was back into theatre to put the tubes back in. After another week they did a scan to check on the bleeding and decided to put a shunt in her head to relieve the pressure, this seemed to help. I knew the doctors were doing all they could for Mum but she was not getting any better.

The next time my Dad saw the surgeon, he told him they would try taking Mum off the life support machine. If she could cope, then they could transfer her back to Blackburn, at least that would make it easier for us to visit. After seven weeks in Preston, Mum was moved to Blackburn, after a week she had her first proper food, a little soup and ice cream, the doctor was pleased with her progress. Another week and the physiotherapist had Mum sitting up in bed, then after a while she could sit in a chair by the bed for an hour.

Now she was trying to eat, Dad would take her a small trifle or Angel Delight for tea, she seemed to like Dad to feed her and she was trying to speak, her mouth would form the words but there was no sound. Then one day when he went to give her a kiss and told her he loved her, she said, "Love you", with a little smile. That was the first time for about nine weeks there had been any response, Dad was so happy when he phoned me that night.

The time leading up to our meeting and me being professed was very difficult for me, I prayed more than ever. My Dad encouraged me that this was right for me, with Mum so ill I suppose what I really wanted was her to say, "Yes Ann, you are ready, it is what you have been working towards."

Saturday July 24th was very special for me. My Dad and friends were at the Mass in St. Joseph's church to witness my Profession into the Third Order of Carmel. I felt at peace, a sense of belonging but also sadness that my dear mother could not be there to see me. Mum had said from the start, "this is for you love, it will happen." Dad and everyone came to congratulate me on taking this final step, saying how sorry they were that Mum could not be with us. When I went to see her in the hospital I told her about my day but I don't know whether she could understand what I said.

Two weeks later it was Mum's birthday, I asked one of the staff to find a nice card and a balloon with 'happy birthday, mum' on for me, I wanted it to be special. Dad had some beautiful flowers, a trifle and lots of cards for her. What a let down! Mum was fast asleep when we went into her room and though I sat talking to her all afternoon, she never once opened her eyes, not until they brought her tea in and sat her up in bed.

The staff began getting Mum out of bed a few hours a day, sitting her in a chair. She was having physiotherapy and had tried speech therapy with no success. They did another scan which Dad told me showed very extensive brain damage and the prognosis was not good at all. The doctor had told my Dad there seemed little hope of any further recovery and advised us to find a nursing home as Mum would require full time nursing now.

This was a very hard blow to take, we knew how ill she was but had always assumed in time she would come home again to have some kind of life with us. Over the next weeks we visited many nursing and care homes, we wanted the very best for her. I was telling Father Michael, our priest, about this when he visited me at Rough Lee. He asked if we had been to Nazareth House, saying it had a very good reputation.

So the following Sunday after Mass we called at Nazareth House. When you walk in there is a lovely feeling of peace and well being all around. Sister Rose-Ann was the first person we saw, she took us into a room to talk about Mum then she showed us around the home. When she took us into their chapel I just said to Dad "this is the place for mum, it is so like Park Place, so peaceful."

Sister Rose-Ann said she would visit mum in hospital and talk to the doctors and staff to see what special needs she'd require, then she would be in touch with us. I felt a lot happier after seeing the home, I just knew she would be well cared for there. A week later everything was arranged and Mum was settled in a lovely room of her own.

I was glad she was on ground level because I could walk in on my own, no wheelchair. What a nice surprise to see her fully dressed, sat in a wheelchair in the lounge with the other residents. At teatime we took her back to her room so that Dad could feed her. Sometimes she would say a few words, she certainly knew when we were there, as soon as she heard my voice her head would turn to me. I don't know if she understood everything I told her but she seemed happy and not in any pain.

The week before Christmas Sister asked if we would like to have Christmas lunch with them? Dad thanked her saying that would be very nice. So we went to Mass with all the residents and friends. Father Cooper, their chaplain, made it a lovely simple Mass for us. When we took Mum to her room Sister had set a table for us with candles, crackers and a bottle of wine, what a wonderful meal we had just the three of us together.

Our lives seemed set in a pattern around Mum. No one could say if there would be any more improvement or how long it would go on. Dad never missed a day visiting her, and the staff were all very good to us. When he went in Zanie, who worked in the dining room, took a tray of tea and cakes for them, I know that they appreciated Dad feeding Mum every day.

I had a letter from Sister Evelyn asking if I would like to spend a week with them in May. I had not been the previous year with Mum being so ill and I did not know what to do. Dad said, "Ann, you always benefit from your stay at Park Place, it will be good for you." I was so glad I took his advice, the Sisters were very pleased to see me and so kind, saying how sorry they were to hear about Mum. Seeing my friends again and talking about Mum helped me come to terms with all that had happened.

Back at Rough Lee we were asked what we would like to do to celebrate the Millennium. Various suggestions were mentioned but the majority were for a trip to Disneyland Paris. Teresa and Sheila arranged everything, finding a coach that would take our wheelchairs and booking the hotel for our three-day stay. We had been hoping to go through the Channel Tunnel but we were not allowed, because of our wheelchairs, so had to cross on the ferry.

We thoroughly enjoyed our stay in a lovely hotel, going on all the different rides at Disneyland, we watched the Grand Parade, which takes place everyday, and then the shows in the evening. What a wonderful experience it was for everyone, we did not want to come home. We thanked Teresa and all the staff and friends who made it possible for us. I had hoped to see something of Paris while we were there but time did not allow, maybe next time.

Another Christmas and New Year spent with Mum in Nazareth House, overall there had been no significant change in her condition. When the weather was warm and sunny we would go for a walk out in the grounds in the sunshine enjoying the fresh air. Mum would say the odd word but always knew when we were with her.

I had become friendly with Pat Taylor, one of the staff there, she asked me one day if I had been to Lourdes, I told her that I had many times, but not recently. She asked me if I would like to go on the Salford Diocesan Pilgrimage, which the bishop leads every year in July.

She said, "Rachel and I will be going with two residents so think about it."

I felt this might be one way I could maybe help my Mum. Visiting Lourdes always gives me a special something, it is hard to explain exactly. I know some people expect a miracle to take place but I don't, for me it is a time to open yourself to Our Lady and ask for her help, it gives me strength to carry on so I can live a better life.

Pat gave me the address of the leader of the group, Father McBride. I wrote telling him about my disability and asking about joining their pilgrimage. He sent me a booking form which Dad helped me fill in and return, a couple of weeks later I had a phone call from a lady called Sylvia asking if she could come and see me.

Sylvia came with another lady, Anne, they were both nurses.

They, along with other doctors and helpers, looked after the sick and disabled pilgrims who stay in the hospital for the week. She asked about my disability, any help I needed and also my medication then she told me about the hospital and the pilgrimage saying, "It's not 'holy, holy', Ann, we have a very good group of young volunteers who look after you and make sure you have fun, I am sure you will enjoy yourself."

That was the start of another lovely friendship, since our first meeting I have been every year and made many friends who regularly keep in touch with me. I certainly feel better having been to Lourdes, I spent a lot of time in prayer with Our Lady and St. Bernadette at the grotto.

The coming year would see changes for us at Rough Lee. The manager, Teresa had been there a very long time and was going to retire at the end of March. The management gave her a farewell party and presentation for all she had done over the years. Residents, staff and many friends all presented her with gifts, wishing her a very happy retirement. Teresa thanked everyone for the gifts and the support she had received, saying she hoped Sheila, who was taking over as manager, would continue the work of the home with the same help she had always been given.

Not long after Sheila had taken over I noticed small changes taking place, we were being more involved in what happened in our home. We were asked about holidays and outings, things we would like to do and also the forming of a family and friends support group. This was a major step forward and brought more people into the home to help us live a normal life.

At the September meeting of the family and friends, the topic of holidays was raised. Sheila said she would like to do something different but the problem was having enough staff to help them. Lucky for us residents, quite a number volunteered their services. Liz, one of the parents, said she would research holidays for the disabled and report back. The outcome was that one group of six residents and six volunteers would fly off to sunny Tenerife at the end of January, and the other group at the end of February. This was certainly something for us to look forward to the following year.

Towards the end of October Mum started with a bad chest infection, we were all very concerned. The doctor called one afternoon while Dad was there and after examining her he told Dad, "Audrey is getting weaker, she has no resistance to fight infection, you should prepare yourself for anything." He put her on antibiotics to help and increased her pain relief medication.

That weekend at home my Dad sat me down and we had a good talk. I suppose, deep down, I always knew Mum would not recover. After nearly four years there had been hardly any change. I had come to terms with the fact that Mum was going to die sooner than I'd expected. Mum did get over that infection but it took a lot out of her and she was now in bed all day.

There had been a change at Nazareth House, Sister Rose-Ann was ill in a Manchester Hospital and Sister Teresa arrived to take charge. As Christmas drew near she told us to carry on as usual and invited us to lunch, "I have been given my instructions" she said, we both thanked her. Mum was a little brighter and managed to sit at the table and eat her meal with us but soon got tired and they put her back into bed.

I felt selfish thinking of my holiday in Tenerife but Dad said, "life goes on love, Mum would not want you to miss this opportunity." We were flying on Friday 31st January, Dad called to see me on Thursday evening after visiting Mum, telling me to have a good time and enjoy myself. He had our hotel number and, if anything happened to Mum, he would let me know, he gave me a big hug and then left.

What a wonderful holiday we had, everyone really enjoyed themselves in the warm sunshine. The hotel was massive, we relaxed by the lovely pool or had a dip in the sea. Good meals, more relaxing then living it up on the town at night. It was our first proper holiday abroad but I am sure we will have many more to look forward to. The only thing was the days flew by and all too soon it was time to come home again. We thanked our volunteers for giving us their time, telling them how much we appreciated all they did for us. Mum had become a lot weaker, not eating much and sleeping more.

I had noticed a big change in her after my holiday. When I came home for the Easter break Dad suggested going to all the services at Nazareth House so we could be near Mum, we wanted to spend as much time as we could there now.

The following weekend when I visited, she looked so poorly. Dad had told me the doctor was calling regularly now and had increased her medication again. She was having difficulty breathing, just gasping for breath, not wanting any food only little drinks. I was very worried about her, before we left I gave her a big kiss and kept looking back at her as I came out of her room, then, in the car going home I burst into tears. I don't think I slept much that night, I cried and prayed for Mum, I did not want her to suffer.

I had just finished my breakfast next morning when I saw Dad's car coming up the drive. I think I knew when I saw the look on his face as he walked into the home. He held me tight saying "I am sorry love, Mum died last night about ten o'clock."

I just screamed then broke my heart as Dad took me to my room. Sheila must have heard me and came in, Dad told her, she was very sorry and said if there was anything she could do to help we had just to ask. He just said, "Please look after Ann, I cannot stay, I have lots of arrangements to make, but I will come back tonight."

That week was very difficult for me, I wanted to be strong for Dad yet all I could think of was the last time I'd seen Mum and how ill she looked. Dad called as often as he could and we sat and talked about Mum's funeral which would take place the following Wednesday. I asked if it could be at Nazareth House and Dad said yes Sister Teresa and Father Copper had been very good helping with the arrangements.

When I came home that weekend and saw all the cards and letters we had received, it made me realise how much people had thought of Mum, there was over sixty. I was dreading the day and seeing Mum's coffin being carried into church, frightened that I would breakdown. On the day my Dad held me close saying "don't worry if you cry Ann, it is nothing to be ashamed of, I will be at your side."

As it was, all went very well, the chapel was full of our friends, Father Copper gave a lovely homely and I only cried a little during the service.

Afterwards Sister Teresa laid a buffet for us, it was good to sit and talk to our friends and relations, especially Mum's brother, Frank and his wife, with us moving away we had not seen them for a long time. All the staff asked us to keep in touch, and we occasionally go to Mass there and have a coffee and a chat.

I had promised Sister Evelyn that I would go and stay again but now I did not know what to do, was it the right thing so soon after Mum's death? I asked Dad who said, "I know how you must be feeling, we have done all we could for Mum. I am sure she would want you to go spend some time with the Sisters, it will help you." Then he decided, as he had not been away for four years, he would come down for a few days, to see his colleagues at the college and stay with Margaret in Winchester.

That week helped me more than anything, being with the Sisters, who were so sorry about Mum, talking about my young life, what I had achieved with Mum's help and my future that lay ahead.

Father Maurice said "You have not lost your mum Ann, she will always be with you only in a different way now."

I had taken my story with me and they all said that I should have it published as it was very good. Dear Sister Evelyn even wrote a lovely dedication for me; *I am dedicating this story to my dear mum in recognition of all the hard work and love she has given me throughout my life.*

~*~

My Dad had phoned Wendy, my social worker, in Winchester to arrange to have my review. She was sorry to hear about Mum and asked me about Rough Lee. I told her about the changes, the holidays and the family support group, she was pleased that I was more settled. Dad said he was happier knowing I had more outside contact and friends than ever, a very good review.

Coming home in the car I told Dad the break had helped sort my mind out, getting things in prospective. I could look forward and have a more positive outlook on my life.

These last chapters of my story have been very difficult for me to write. Margaret my friend in Winchester told me that it was something I had to do, bring all my thoughts out on paper and see it in print. She said I would find that it would give me great relief and it has.

God Bless you Mum. I will never forget you.

**More great books from
Mediaworld and Best Books Online
can be seen on our publishing web site at
www.bestbooksonline.co.uk**

Publish with us in electronic book form
traditional form, or both and
your work receives world-wide listings.

**E-mail publishing@bestbooksonline.net
or call us on
0845 1661104 within the United Kingdom, or
+447092103738 from outside
(24 hour voicemail facility)**

**Mediaworld PR Ltd,
Yeadon, Leeds,
West Yorkshire.
Words and people that mean business**

We are a specialist company offering
much more than traditional publishers.
We deal with our authors personally
and provide all editing and marketing services
on a one to one basis.

WITHDRAWN